The Romance of
Saskatchewan
Settlements

by
Colin A. Thomson and Rodney G. Thomson

ISBN 0-9734313-0-X

Published by
THORO Publishing
678-21st Street East
Prince Albert, Saskatchewan, Canada
S6V 1M7
Phone: (306) 763-3350   Fax: (306) 763-5602
Email: thoropublishing@yahoo.ca

Printed by
Ultra Print Services Ltd, North Battleford, Saskatchewan, Canada

DEDICATION

This work is dedicated to
Glen C. Thomson (1900-1978)
and
Vera M. (Whenham) Thomson (1904-1994)

The authors gratefully acknowledge the technical assistance of Jim White, Wayne Hawthorne and Eleanor Thomson.

About the Authors

The Thomson brothers, Depression Babies born and raised in Ridgedale, share a deep love for their home province, Saskatchewan. With countless others, they look forward to the province's 100th birthday celebrations in 2005.

Colin, University of Lethbridge historian and Professor Emeritus, has served universities in Saskatoon, Lethbridge, Kenya, Lesotho and Nigeria. Earlier he served a number of Saskatchewan school districts. The ex-oil rigger, construction worker, hail adjuster, pipe line worker, and handy man (a skill in dispute), shares three children and six grandchildren with his wife Eleanor (Hunter). He is the author of six books and numerous academic papers. A novel based in the prairies is now in progress.

Rod is retired from teaching in Prince Albert and this book represents his second effort in writing and research. He had a broad career in education, social work, alcoholism counselling, outfitting and politics. He is retired from Prince Albert City Council but currently serves as a trustee with Saskatchewan Rivers School Board. He and his wife Valerie (McBrien) have a married daughter in Saskatoon. He is currently compiling and editing a snapshot history of schools in 1954 to be released soon.

They are proud of the Canadian heritage they have traced to the original settlers of Scarborough, Ontario in 1796, David Thomson and Mary Glendenning and their eleven children.

TABLE OF CONTENTS

AUTHORS' NOTE

The pictures of collapsing grain elevators are depressing and cause for nostalgia. Similar events have taken place in hundreds of western Canadian communities. The destruction of the "prairie pyramids" of Saskatchewan at the end of the 20th Century and later marks the change from a predominantly agricultural province to a province with a diversified economy. Perhaps even more dramatic has been the rapid urbanization of the population and in many cases the disappearance of a way of life.

At one time there were six thousand of these structures and now there may be ten percent of that. Like these landmarks, many early settlements or "post offices" have disappeared. The crashing elevator is graphically symbolic of a changing Saskatchewan landscape. Not only was Saskatchewan, but the three prairie provinces were populated from border to border with these symbols of agricultural strength. The first Saskatchewan rectangular elevator was built at Indian Head in 1883. By 1920 there were two thousand of them throughout the west and by 1938 there were nearly six thousand across the prairies. Today there are probably fewer than six hundred.

Many Saskatchewan settlements and their elevators were named in honour of "*people of the pen*" – writers, poets, journalists, scientists, jurists, historians, diplomats, dramatists, artists, composers, architects, humourists, philosophers, educators, among others. The authors of this book believe that our pioneers chose well in the naming of their communities in honour of those learned, talented and energetic men and women whose warts and halos are in clear sight.

The demise of these "prairie pyramids" has paralleled the demise of many of the early settlements, settlements that had a romance that must be preserved as

Saskatchewan celebrates its one-hundredth year in 2005. There are many ghost towns that carry with their memory stories of people who laboured to develop this vast land.

The traveller who takes the Trans-Canada Highway from Fleming near the Manitoba border to Walsh near the Alberta border, sees about five hundred miles of flatland. Those travellers do not see 125,000 square miles of forest, water, desert, sand dunes, rock and tundra. They would be surprised to learn of 15,000 square miles of water surface with some 100,000 lakes. This represents the "other half" of a province misunderstood, mysterious in many ways, and creative in the naming of its communities.

This book will explore the lives of those people of the arts community whose names identified the communities of the province. Many of these communities have disappeared with "progress" so the preservation of the Saskatchewan heritage becomes the priority of this study.

Photo courtesy of Kent Jones, Prince Albert

SASKATCHEWPENS: WHAT A PROVINCE!

What can be said about a province that has Romance, Cupid, Love and Honeymoon? And Insight? Add Livelong. And Diana. (She was the Roman goddess, who lived in perpetual celibacy, presided over childbirth and, as the hunters may know, was also the goddess of the chase.)

Where else can you find a Canuck, Union Jack, New Ottawa, Red Cross and Adanac? (Spell it backwards.) Where else would you find Tangleflags, so named to honour the many ethnic groups who homesteaded in that area northeast of Lloydminister?

What would outsiders think when they first hear of such Saskatchewan places as Boundary, Broadview, Buttress, Climax, Conquest, Endeavor, Foreward, Friend, Landscape, Liberty, Lonesome Butte, Onward, Outlook, Paradise Hill, Peerless, Pleasantdale, Plenty, Reliance, Revenue, Richmound, Ridgedale, Sanctuary, Scentgrass, Sonningdale, Stalward, Steepes, Strong, Strongfield, Success, Sunkist, Sunny Glen, Sunnyvale, Superb, Supreme, Tableland, Tallpines, Unity, Valor, Vanguard, Viewfair, Vigilant, Westhope, Wideview, Yellowgrass, amongst others?

Imagine going to Hak to find a place named after a railway official by the name of H.A.K. Drury.

Can you name four dozen communities in Saskatchewan named after our wildlife? How many are named after native flowers, trees, shrubs?

How many Indian names and words are found on a map of Saskatchewan? Do you recognize Meetoos, Witchekan, Wiwa, Akosane, Waskesiu among many more?

In the "Land of the Living Skies" women held up half that sky but perhaps only three percent of the provincial communities are named for females. How complete is this list? Alida, Alma, Amelia, Annaheim, Arabella, Baljennie, Beadle, Beaubier, Belbutte, Blewett, Cater, Catherwood,

Cavell, Charlotte, Charmian, Constance, Corinne, Deborah, Diana, Dorintosh, Emma Lake, Emmaville, Ethelton, Glen Mary, Grace, Grandora, Idalene, Junor, Lydden, Lady Lake, Lake Lenore, Laura, Loverna, Madge Lake, Margo, Maryfield, Marysburg, Maryville, Maymont, Megan, Melba, Mildred, Milly, Nora, Nashlyn, Notukeu (Cree for Old Woman), Pickthall, Robsart, Rosemae, Ruthilda, Semans, Sisley, Squaw Rapids (E.B. Campbell Hyro Electric Station), Stelcam, St. Marguerite, Una, Val Marie, Vera, Verwood, Victoire, Victoria Plains, Vidora, Viola, Vonda, Winside, Yonker, Zelma. Would you include Regina, "The Queen City"? And what about Bonne Madone? (Good Lady) And would you include Old Wives, named in honour of those courageous Cree women who fell to the Blackfoot so that the rest of their hunting party and children could escape with their buffalo harvest?

St. Walburg, St. Louis, St. Marguerite, St. Laurent were named for Saints. Name at least a dozen more "saint" centres.

Obviously many centres were named after places in other provinces, USA, Great Britain and continental Europe. Togo, Fukushiama, and Kuroki provide the Japanese "connection." There are at least two centres with an Egyptian connection: Khedive (earlier Governor or Viceroy) and Charmain (Cleopatra's faithful servant who followed her queen to death by suicide.) Two other centres, Eyre and Zealandia, provide a New Zealand connection. Kandahar was named for the battle of Kandahar, Afghanistan. Viceroy received its name from the title "Viceroy of India." (The town has six streets named after six individuals who served in that capacity.) Freemantle got its name from an Australian centre. Java is named after an island now part of Indonesia.

Among others, the following places are named for military leaders: Arburthnot, Blucher, Braddock, Dollard, Eyre, Keppel, Ketchen, Lepine, Ormeaux, Redvers, Smuts, Sturdee, Togo, Tuxford, Wauchope, Wolsely, Wolfe. (Many centres were named for Canadian servicemen killed in two world wars, the Boer War and conflicts in India.) It seems very likely that Findlater was named for George Findlater who won the Victoria Cross for great courage during the 1898 attack on Dargai Heights, India. How many other provinces have so honoured a V.C winner?

Famous battles are noted by Amiens, Crecy, Dunkirk, Lancer, Louvain, Major, Marengo, Naseby, Plassey, Somme and Valor add flavour to that list. (1)

Did you know that the communities of Maxim and Marlin are named after guns?

You find a biblical connection with Cana, Carmel, Ebenezer, Galilee, and Jordan River.

Coronach was named after a horse, an Epson Down winner. At least four communities have "horse" in their names. Can you name them?

Tiny was named after a dog.

Loreburn, Phippen, Duff, Landis, Viscount, Dummer, Prendergast, Richardson, and Rouleau were named after judges.

Macoun, Wollaston Lake, Kelvington, Herschel, Humboldt, amongst others, were named for famous scientists.

Saskatchewan has many communities and centres named for politicians, Canadian and non-Canadian. Consider Asquith, Baldwinton, Barbour, Borden, Bracken, Burrows, Calder, Caron, Cazalet, Chamberlain, Clemenceau, Craigavon, Craven, Curzon, Davis, Dilke, Dorintosh, Douglaston, Dubuc, Duncairn, Dunning, Fielding, Fort Pitt, Haultain, Havalin, Hazenmore, Herbert, Holmes, Insinger, Knollys, Laird, Lepine, Loreburn, MacDowall, MacNutt,

(1) One wonders if any Canadian community could equal the ratio of men who served in World War I. At least four dozen Alingly (N.W. of Prince Albert) men served in that conflict. Fourteen of them are buried in France. Another question: Why didn't Alingly, named for a village in southern England, have its name changed to Sacrifice, Patriotville or...?

Madison, McAra, McGee, Norquay, Parkerview, Percival, Prince, Pym, Runciman, Rutan, Smeaton, Smuts, Sutherland, Totzke, Traux, Walpole, Watson, Weirdale, Windthorst, Woodrow.

At least three communities were named for people who were shot dead: Cavell, (2) Percival, (3) and McGee. (4) Several centres were named for drowning victims. Another, Crichton, was named for a man killed in a brawl. Other centres were named after people who committed suicide. e.g. Davin and Tannahill.

How many places can you list that were named after clergymen, missionaries, railway workers and executives, farmers, and ranchers? And prospectors, business people, police, educators, surveyors, doctors, postmasters, bankers?

Altawan, Alsask, and Mantario "identify" a relationship with other provinces. Any other examples?

Which towns would you like to drive around? In Cadillac, or Chrysler? Cadillac has a Ford and Essex Street.

Do you feel you are with a King's or Queen's representative when you visit Aberdeen, Laird, Earl Grey (who gave us CFL football's championship cup), Bulyea, Forget, Aikins, Tweedsmuir?

There are a few "Fort" places in Saskatchewan. e.g. Fort Walsh, Fort Pitt, Fort a la Corne, Fort San, Fort Black, Fort Qu'Appelle. Can you name others?

Is not Wakaw the only town whose spelling forms a palindrome. Spell it frontwards and backwards.

(2)   The Red Cross nurse served in Belgium during WW I. She helped Allied soldiers to escape from behind enemy lines. The Germans caught, tried and executed her in 1915. As nurse Edith Cavell was led to the firing squad she said; "I realize that patriotism is not enough; I must have no hatred or bitterness toward anyone." Alberta's Mount Edith Cavell is named in her honour. (Cavell is west of Landis.)

(3)   In the lobby of the House of Commons, British Prime Minister Percival (1809-1812) was shot to death by John Bellingham, a "broker gone broke." Bellingham was surely insane but he was hanged in any case. (Percival is near Broadview.)

(4)   McGee's assassination is discussed elsewhere in this book.

Can you add to this list of Saskatchewan places named in honour of explorers, frontiersmen, mapmakers? e.g. Batoche, Bridger, Cadillac, Camsell, Codette, Drake, Fort a la Corne, Frobisher, Hearne, Pambrun, Pangman, Radisson, Shackelton, Simpson, Turner Lake, Verendrye? Did you know that Strehlow, near Dundurn, was the home of Charles Palmer, a former member of the infamous Jesse James gang? Palmer had notches cut on his rifle, had a price on his head in USA, and kept his distance from his neighbours. When the rancher-cobbler died in 1916, he was nearly one-hundred years old. Why isn't there a Palmerville in the province? Such is notoriety.

Shouldn't someone build a miniature Stonehenge near Stonehenge, Saskatchewan?

Shouldn't a statue be made in Lashburn to honour Laura Sisley who brought many downtrodden English boys to Saskatchewan? An earlier post office and a baptismal font were named for this remarkable individual.

Is there a "bigger name" in Saskatchewan than Louis Riel? What else, if anything, should be named or created in his honour? (The major north-south highway was recently named the Louis Riel Trail.) Where is the statue of Edith Cavell? Of a Miss H. Beaubier, a young teacher who lost her life while looking after victims of the 1918 flu epidemic? (Beaubier, named after the teacher's honour, is west of Estevan.)

Isn't Hinchcliff the only Saskatchewan centre named for a commercial pilot? Hinchcliff, in 1930, flew the first England-to-America airplane passengers. Endeavour, near Sturgis, was named after the airplane.

Is Outram the only Saskatchewan district named after a mountaineer who was the first to climb some of the highest peaks in the Canadian Rockies?

Landlocked Saskatchewan named Titanic, a post office near Carlton, after the famous ship that sank to the Atlantic's bottom on the night of April 14-15, 1912.

Supposedly the 882 foot vessel carrying 2500 passengers was unsinkable. One of the victims was the Grand Trunk Railway president, Charles Melville Hays, after whom Melville, Saskatchewan was named. (The province also has a Neptune, named for the Roman god of the sea.) Lac Vert and Green Lake are both in Saskatchewan. How many places have "gold" in their name? e.g. Goldburg, Goldburn, Golden Prairie. How many have "glen" in their name? e.g. Glen Elder, Glenavon, Fairy Glen. How many have "rose" in their name? e.g. Rose Valley, Rosetown.

A surveyor's mistake led to the name of the hamlet Cosine, near the Alberta border. Logarithm tables can be a problem?

Railway surveyor Miles Patrick Cotton had each of his three names attached to communities near Lipton. (McGee and D'Arcy, Bryant and Cullen, Plunkett and Viscount, Henribourg and Albertville are all two-place names honouring one individual.)

Congress is just north of Assiniboia. Officials correctly assumed that the name would attract American settlers who were to see their streets get such names as North Lincoln Road, Washington Avenue, Hughes Street, Taft Road, East Roosevelt Avenue, among others.

Anti-German sentiment was high during the First World War and many communities went through a change of name. Well known was Berlin, Ontario which became Kitchener. In Saskatchewan, the switch was widespread:

New Name	Original	New Name	Original
Bethune	Waldorf	Raymore	Wolfsheim
Burstall	Schmidt	Rhine	Rheine
Cavell	Coblenz	Scottsguard	Kramer
Edenwold	New Tulcea	Sedley	New Holstein
Killaly	Mareahilf	Simmie	Maescow
Kroneau	Kathherenthal	Springside	Leckmann
Langenburg	Hokenloke	Strasbourg	New Elsace
Leader	Prussia	Vibank	Alsace
Peebles	Kaiser	Young	Eigenheim

An interesting development in the place names of Saskatchewan communities is the area this book refers to as Writers Corner. In an area roughly from Moose Jaw south of #1 Highway and east is that portion of the province that has many communities that have honoured people of the pen. They are all here and this book is dedicated to those community names that are associated with the arts. Many of these names were once emblazoned on the grain elevators, the "prairie pyramids," and like those landmarks, too many have disappeared into history. This book is dedicated to the preservation of those settlements, communities that extend from Wallaston in the north to the USA border, an area larger than many nations and most states in the USA.

The authors recognize the geographical centre of the province as Mulanosa and that the maps following represent the lower, southern portion of the province.

Saskatchewan South-West
Locate Chrichton, Ferland, Masefield, Pickthall, Tannahill, Robsart, and Valjean.

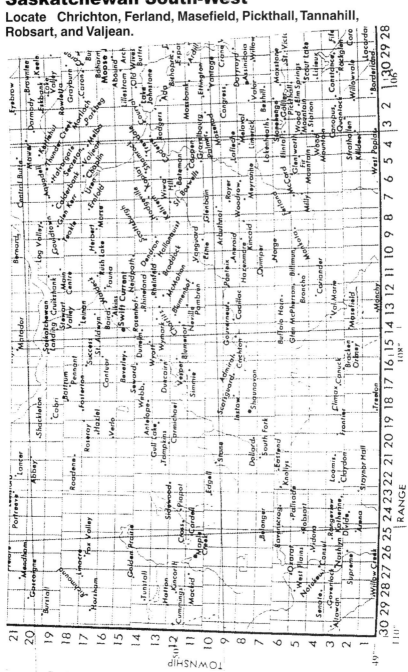

Saskatchewan South-East

WRITERS CORNER: Readers are invited to locate Avonlea, Bengough, Blewett, Browning, Bryant, Carlyle, Cowper, Cullen, Davin, Dumas, Dummer, Fleming, Froude, Gainsborough, Hardy, Hume, Ibsen, Kipling, Lampman, Luxton, Macoun, Mair, Maxwelton, Parkman, Pitman, Richardson, Rouleau, Ryerson, Service, Trossachs, and Wordsworth.

Saskatchewan North-East

Find Bagley, Coxby, Cudworth, Curzon, Dafoe, Dana, Dilke, Drake, Duff, Elstow, Garrick, Holbein, Humboldt, Kelvington, Ituna, Lipton, Nokomis, Mozart, Runnymede, Southey, and Wollaston.

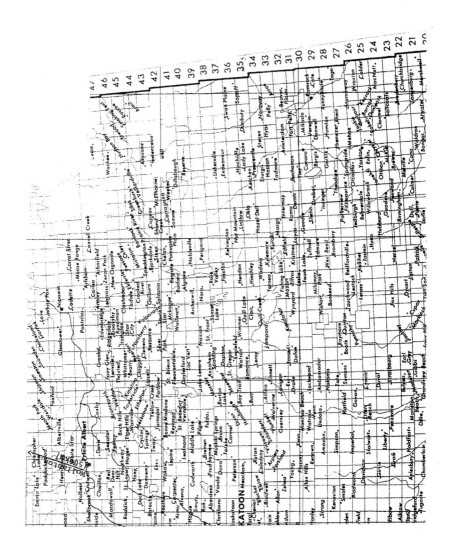

Saskatchewan North-West

Here you will locate Ardath, D'Arcy, McGee, Handel, Herschel, Isham, Luxton, Minnehaha, Prendergast, Richard, Ridpath, Robinhood, Roddick, Swinbourne, Thackeray, and Esk

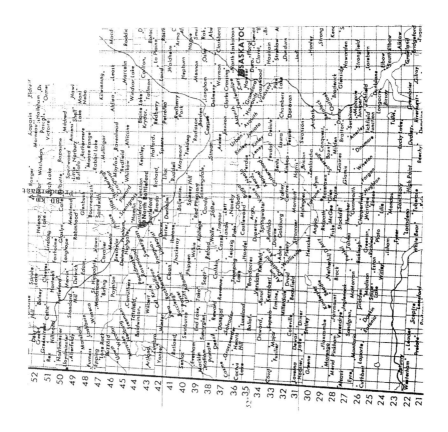

ARDATH

Cross the South Saskatchewan at Outlook and head a bit west, then north to Ardath, named for a book written by the fascinating and infuriating Marie Corelli. Avoid any small woman with Shetland ponies and a gondola.

MARIE CORELLI (1855-1924)

Marie Corelli (pseudonym for Marie "Minnie" MacKay), all four feet ten inches of her, wielded a very busy pen. Many experts claim that she was the best selling author in the world for nearly thirty years. Some of Corelli's romantic and melodramatic novels went into fiftieth and sixtieth editions. During every year of her writing career her publishers sold more than 100,000 copies of her books.

So popular was her writing that thousands waited outside her lecture rooms, and some fought to touch her gown. Corelli's admirers included the famous, and she openly courted their favour, often to their embarrassment. She loved the limelight and publicity. The Englishwoman moved to Stratford-on-Avon where she tried to associate her reputation with that of Shakespeare.

The productive writer had an image of herself-a coy and childlike young maiden-even after she became quite overweight. In 1902 she purchased two Shetland ponies and a miniature cart which was to carry her and her large friend, Bertha Vyver with whom, some claim, she had a lesbian relationship for many years. She decorated the cart with fancy bells and silver lamps, and dressed herself in bow-trimmed, ruffled girl-like clothing. Later she purchased a Venice gondola and hired a uniformed gondolier who took the two women on the Avon River.

Corelli's books were outrageously overwritten, loved by many readers and scorned by most critics. With her pages loaded with adverbs, adjectives, many clichés, archaisms and repetitions she scolded women who rode bicycles, smoked cigarettes, supported socialism or the suffragette movement, among other "errors". Her literary intensity is found in the love scenes which placed the lovers in strange, exotic and often bizarre settings. Yet she found it difficult to use such words as bosom, stomach, leg or breast.

It is claimed that at age fifty-one, Corelli had a brief affair with the artist Arthur Severn, very married for forty years and a father of five grown children. Corelli wrote letters to him using baby talk, now embarrassing to some readers. She believed that women are born to "lift men a step nearer to glory." Those men must not make a woman a scapegoat after they "devour her by selfish lust."

A mixture of spiritualism, offensive sentimentalism, religious bigotry and prejudice is found in Corelli's works. It has been suggested that it is very difficult to find another notoriously bad writer whose books were so widely read.

Today, some readers find Corelli's writing quaint and amusing. Others find her wordiness and passion to be contemptible. Consider these lines from *Ardath:*

> *Night was approaching, though away to the west a broad gash of crimson, a seeming wound in the breast of heaven, showed where the sun had set an hour since. Now and again the rising wind moaned sobbingly through the tall and spectral pines that, with knotted roots fast clenched in the reluctant earth, clung tenaciously to their stony vantage ground; and mingling with its wailing murmur, there came a distant hoarse roaring as of tumbling torrents, while at far-off intervals could be heard the sweeping thud of an avalanche slipping from point to point on its disastrous downward way.... Gradually the wind increased, and soon with sudden fierce gusts shook the pine trees into shuddering anxiety—the red slit in the sky closed...then—with a swirling, hissing rush of rain—the unbound hurricane burst forth alive and furious...the tempest rolled, thundered and shrieked its way....*

Perhaps her most famous works are *A Romance of Two Worlds* (dealing with psychic experience), *Barrabbas: A Dream of the World's Tragedy* (a story of Christ's crucifixion), *The Sorrows of Satan* (another religious theme) and *The Murder of Delicia*.

More insight can be gained from this comment by the productive Marie Corelli:

> *I never married because there was no need. I have three pets at home which serve the same purpose as a husband. I have a dog which growls every morning, a parrot which swears all afternoon and a cat that comes home late at night.*

Critics continue to blast Corelli for what they consider bad taste and sickening sentimentality.

AVONLEA

Because a number of Lucy Maud Montgomery's relatives lived nearby, the settlement was named in honour of her fictional Anne of Avonlea.

Take highway #6 south from Regina to the Corinne corner. Drive west on #334 for twenty minutes or so to Avonlea.

Watch for a freckled, red-haired, energetic girl who will steal your heart.

Should Avonlea be declared "Canadian capital of Writers Corner"?

LUCY MAUD MONTGOMERY (1874-1942)

Just think of all the television shows, books, souvenirs, trinkets, dolls and tourist dollars that have been spun from a story of a freckled-faced, red-haired Canadian girl called Anne of Green Gables, the literary creation of Lucy Maud Montgomery, the daughter of an ex-sea captain and his wife, Clara.

When Clara died, the grief-stricken father sent his two-year-old daughter, Maud, to live with her elderly, strictly Presbyterian maternal grandparents who lived in rural Prince Edward Island. There, the imaginative, sensitive Maud found that writings by Scott, Byron, Dickens, among others, could give her some respite from her lonely life. Maud also had many friends and cousins in rural Prince Edward Island.

In 1890, Maud's father remarried and with his family moved to Prince Albert, Saskatchewan. She and her step-mother did not get along well in that western settlement. However, in that year Maud had a poem published in a Prince Edward Island paper. That event excited her so the young Maud moved back to that province the following year.

Maud, in 1893, prepared for a teaching career by attending the Prince of Wales College in Charlottetown. She found less satisfaction in her three-year teaching career than she did in her writing that she did in her spare time.

The strong-willed, intelligent, ambitious young woman was very feminine, as she might describe herself. She knew that men admired her slim good looks and charming personality. She had serious romantic attachments with at least two young gentlemen before realizing that she should not look foreword to romantic love.

For some time the writer lived with and cared for her grandmother in Cavendish, on the Island. She carried on a long correspondence with a Scottish journalist and a Canadian teacher, Ephraim Weber.

In 1907, Maud's oft-rejected novel, *Anne of Green Gables*, was published in Boston. Anne, a red-headed, irrepressible girl, caught the public's fancy. As Maud once said, "Anne seems to have hit the public taste." Among the fan letters Maud received was one from Mark Twain who described Anne as "the dearest and most loveable child in fiction since the immortal Alice [in Wonderland]."

A sequel. *Anne of Avonlea* followed in 1909. In all, there were eight Anne books that meant that Maud's professional and financial status was assured.

After her grandmother died in 1911, Maud, after a secret, five-year engagement, married Ewan MacDonald, an amiable Presbyterian minister. They had their honeymoon in the British Isles before settling in Leaksdale, Ontario. The couple had two sons, Chester and Stuart.

Maud's husband later suffered mental problems and she was engaged in expensive, acrimonious lawsuits with her publisher. The family moved to Norval, Ontario where Maud wrote the popular *Emily of New Moon.*

World War II distressed Maud and her husband. Both suffered breakdowns in the 1930's and early 1940's. In spite of these problems, Maud was named a fellow of the Royal Society of Arts in Scotland, and in 1935 she was invested with the *Order of the British Empire.* Maud's books continued to sell. Included are her autobiography, 430 poems, 500 short stories, and 22 books of fiction.

Today, Lucy Maud Montgomery, *Anne of Green Gables*, and *Anne of Avonlea* have become literary icons. And has Prince Edward Island ever been the same?

BAGLEY

Drive north and a little east from Melfort to Gronlid. Stop. You have gone too far. Your destination, Bagley, was a post office south-west, a stamp away.

Reflect on your school days. What made your favourite teacher your favourite? Or most effective? Are you "strapped" for an answer?

WILLIAM CHANDLER BAGLEY (1874-1946)

If you make the following speech to local students and teachers will you be cheered or hissed? You will not be ignored!

"Ladies and Gentlemen-teachers and students. Education is in trouble but I have solutions and plans for excellence. Allow me to list my ideas in point form.

1) *We need an Essentialist"s Platform for education: We require the firm facts of the physical and social sciences as the basis of subject matter which all students must acquire.*
2) *Schools shouldn't spend so much time satisfying individual interests and desires. Instead schools must pass on the accepted values of society as well as the realities of scientific fact.*
3) *It is time to reassert the values of discipline, authority, tradition and scientific truth. That is the conservative function of education.*
4) *Mathematical and language skills are the essentials upon which any curriculum must be built.*
5) *The "soft" pedagogy of the so-called progressive education movement is still with us. It must be replaced with the Essentialist Program.*
6) *Science rather than narrow psychological studies must be the foundation of good teaching.*
7) *The ultimate aim of education is efficiency, that is, social efficiency. Result: The development of the socially efficient individual.*
8) *An efficient school system requires "unquestioned obedience" of teachers and students to the authority of the principal and the superintendent. The principal is like the captain of a ship who issues orders (i.e. the course of study) to the teachers who in turn make sure all students master the required skills and knowledge. Some latitude will be granted if deserved.*
9) *As suggested earlier, for effective teaching it is necessary that an adequate conception of principles based on the best data science can offer be added to a mastery of technique.*
10) *It is essential to determine the scientific theoretical basis for the professionalization of teacher education.*

Thank you for your attention."

Those ten points do scant justice to the thinking of William Chandler Bagley, educator and theorist.

The Detroit-born William, a good student, attended local schools and then the Michigan Agricultural College. After graduation he taught in a one-room school in Garth, a lumber community. Then he began University of Chicago studies in education and learning theory before returning for a second stint at Garth's school. In 1900 he completed his PhD in education. He accepted an elementary principalship in St. Louis where he met and married Florence MacLean Winger. (They were to have four children.) For several years he served as professor and director of teacher training at the Montana State Normal College at Dillon when he was also school superintendent.

In 1909 Bagley was appointed professor and director of the School of Education at the University of Illinois. Eight years later he moved to Teachers College, Columbia University in New York. For the next two decades and more he continued his studies of schooling and teacher education.

Bagley's writings, articles and books were very influential. His textbook *Classroom Management* (1907) was considered a guide for beginning teachers. Over 100,000 books were sold and it remained in print until 1946. Other Bagley books were used in teacher education classes: *The Educative Process* (1905) and *Educational Values* (1911), among others. He helped to form several educational journals and served as consultant to school districts. With historian Charles A. Beard he wrote the *History of the American People*.

Today many people dismiss Bagley's ideas which seemingly don't fit today's "life style"—whatever that means. If Bagley was wrong, then who is correct? Was Bagley's pen pointed in the wrong direction? Why or why not?

BENGOUGH

Take Highway #6 south from Regina to Ceylon, and then turn west for the thirty minute drive to the community called Bengough, named for a cartoonist. Check the locals in this part of Writers Corner for their sense of humour and for their faith in "established politicians".

THOMAS WILSON BENGOUGH (1851-1923)

Perhaps the only Saskatchewan centre named after a cartoonist is Bengough. The gifted political cartoonist helped greatly to create the "picture" accepted by many of the first Prime Minister, John A. Macdonald.

The Prime Minister's whiskey nose, slyness, and wit were confirmed by Bengough's artistic talent. In many ways he can be considered a 19th Century Canadian social radical because of his interests: prohibition, feminism, vegetarianism, antivivisectionalism and communalism. Later he returned to journalism (He started with George Brown's *Globe* in 1871 but left to form and edit his *Grip*, a satirical weekly 1873-1894.) and to the lecture tour. In 1974 selections of his *Caricature History of Canadian Politics* (1886) were reprinted.

Bengough was a campaigner, journalist, reporter, communicator, poet, artist and a formidable critic (and thorn in the side) of the established order. But he was best known as a cartoonist and wit. Few Canadians have "laughed louder" at politicians. Although he often made light of the problems of the day, he also offered his "solutions" to those problems.

Perhaps no one more strongly supported the concept and practice of "the single tax"-the idea that a single tax upon the value of land should eclipse all other taxes and

WE IN CANADA SEEM TO HAVE LOST ALL IDEA OF JUSTICE, HONOR AND INTEGRITY — The Mail, 20th September.

become the government's only source of revenue. Bengough convinced few people on that topic.

Some of Bengough's solutions were couched in his colourful language:

-His [George Brown] was a rushing mountain stream;
His faults but eddies which its swiftness bred.
-The curse [whiskey] of Canada.
-The traitor's hand is at thy throat,
Ontario! Ontario!
Then kill the tyrant with thy vote,
Ontario! Ontario!

BLEWETT

West of Lampman is the community called Blewett, named after the brilliant poetess, Jean Blewett. Watch for cornflowers. After all, *Cornflowers* is one of her most beautiful poems. Blewett: Worthy member of Writers Corner.

JEAN BLEWETT (1862-1934)

John and Janet Blewett (nee McIntyre) of Scotia, Canada West, realized early that their daughter Jean was an exceptional child. The popular, clever girl was educated at St. Thomas Collegiate Institute. At age seventeen, she married Bassett Blewett of Cornwall, Ontario. For many years she contributed articles to the Toronto *Globe*. Later she became a full-time staff member. (Not many other female contemporaries were allowed or encouraged to join the professions.) She advanced to the editorship of the Homemaker's Department of the Toronto newspaper. Blewett retired from active journalism in 1925.

Throughout her marriage she spent her "spare time" writing, reading and discussing the issues of the day. In 1890 she published her first and only novel, *Out of the Depths*. She published several volumes of poetry: *Heart Songs* (1897), *The Cornflower and Other Poems* (1906) and *Poems* (1922). One of her poems, *Spring*, captured the six-hundred dollar prize offered by the *Chicago Times Herald*.

Globe magazine commented on Blewett's work:

She deals with homely subjects in a homely way. She does not attempt wild flights of rhapsody or deep philosophical problems. It is an everyday sort of poetry, simple in theme and treatment, unpretentious, domestic, kindly, humorous and natural.... In sentiment and in morals her poems are wholesome and, to use feminine adjective, 'sweet....' Her lessons are of self-denial and of the power of love to mould men and women.

Perhaps Blewett's *At Quebec* best illustrates her sense of history and her sensitivity:

QUEBEC, the grey old city on the hill,
Lies with a golden glory on her head,
Dreaming throughout this hour so fair-so still-
Of other days and all her might dead.
The white doves perch upon the cannons grim,
The flowers bloom where once did run a tide
Of crimson, when the moon rose pale and dim
Above the battlefield so grim and wide.
Methinks within her wakes a mighty glow
Of pride, of tenderness-her stirring past-
The strife, the valour, of long ago
Feels at her heartstrings. Strong, tall, and vast,
She lies, touched with the sunset's golden grace,
A wondrous softness on her grey old face.

Blewett's sense of fun is found in *The Boy of the House*. (1897)

There's two of twins – oh, it must be fun
To go double at everything,
To holler by twos, and to run by twos,
To whistle by twos and to sing!

Everyday happenings were faithfully described by the poetess. For example, in *She Just Keeps House for Me*, she wrote:

Our children climb upon her knee
And lie upon her breast,
And ah! Her mission seems to me
The highest and the best;
And so I say with pride untold,
And love beyond degree,
This woman with the heart of gold
She just keeps house for me.

Her *Chore Time* appeals to all of us with rural backgrounds.

Jean Blewett's work should be better known in Canada. Consider:

Sweet is the earth when the summer is young,
And the barley fields are green and gold.

One would think that she was talking about the area around Blewett, Saskatchewan. Also consider:

The harvest sun lay hot and strong
On waving grain and grain in sheaf,
On dusty highway stretched along,
On hill and vale, on stalk and leaf.

BROWNING

If you enjoy love stories then you will want to read about Elizabeth's and Robert's genuine affection-yes, adoration for each other. A bit north of Estevan is the Browning settlement, named after poet Robert Browning. Writers Corner again honours a literary talent that endures and inspires.

ROBERT BROWNING (1812-1889)

Browning, a major English poet of the Victorian era, noted for his mastery of psychological portraiture and dramatic monologue, (e.g. *My Last Duchess*) was born in a London suburb of well-to-do parentage. He had private tutors as well as instruction from his father rather than regular schooling. His mother influenced his love for music, his interest in flora and fauna, and his religion. It is claimed that young Robert read all six thousand books-printed in several languages-in his father's library. The brilliant Robert left university early to travel on the continent. "Italy was my university," said Robert Browning.

In 1844, Browning wrote a letter of congratulations to Elizabeth Barrett on her new book of poems. She replied, triggering an exchange over the next twenty months of nearly six hundred letters. She was thirty-eight, an invalid dependent on morphine to ease the pain, and he was thirty-two, a struggling poet.

In 1846 Robert secretly married Elizabeth Barrett whose literary fame at the time was far greater than his. After they eloped she wrote her brother that despite "my ghastly face," Browning "made me feel with every breath I drew in his presence, that he loved me with no ordinary affection." A week later they left for Italy where they remained for most of their married life.

It must be noted that Elizabeth suffered severe health problems, likely a result of an early riding accident. Her courtship with Robert was kept a close secret from her domineering, despotic father of whom she stood in fear. In spite of her semi-invalidism, she wrote love poems (e.g. *Sonnets From the Portuguese*) which were inspired by her love for her husband. What demonstrates love more than her sonnet *How Do I Love Thee*?

How do I love thee? Let me count the ways.
I love thee to the depth and breadth and height
My soul can reach, when feeling out of sight
For the ends of Being and ideal Grace.

13

I love thee to the level of every day's
Most quiet need, by sun and candlelight.
I love thee freely, as men strive for Right;
I love thee purely, as they turn from Praise;
I love thee with the passion put to use
In my old griefs, and with my childhood's faith;
I love thee with a love I seemed to lose
With my lost saints,-I love thee with the breath,
Smiles, tears, of all my life! -and, if God choose,
I shall but love thee better after death.

Robert's fame was slow to arrive. His early work included poetic tragedies and several that received faint praise from critics. However, his love lyrics written during his marriage to Elizabeth were among the most beautiful poems he produced. Those lyrics are musical and delightfully simple. He achieved great fame later in life when he came to be ranked with Alfred, Lord Tennyson.

Shortly before his marriage to Elizabeth he asked himself a question: "What will be the event of my love for her?" He randomly opened a book and his eyes caught one sentence: "If we love in the other world as we do in this, I shall love thee to eternity." But this was the same Robert who was cornered at a party by a talkative, boring man. "But my dear fellow, this is too bad. I am monopolizing you," he stated and fled.

The optimism of Browning is captured in his *Pippa Passes*.

The year's at the spring
And the day's at the morn;
Morning's at seven;
The hill-side's dew-pearled;
The lark's on the wing;
The snail's on the thorn:
God's in his heaven-
All's right with the world!

Perhaps his oft-quoted "Ah, but a man's reach should exceed his grasp, or what's a heaven for?" says it better.

Browning's optimism and vigorous statements of faith continue to inspire. So does his bold energy of expression. Example: "Who knows but the world may end tonight."

On the 28th day of June, 1861 the world of Elizabeth ended. She was unaware of her danger and assured her beloved husband that she was better-much better. Her last words were from a poem: "Knowledge by suffering endureth. And life is perfected by death." All through the night her husband watched alone as the breath of the sleeper went and came more and more softly. At daytime he bent closer to listen and wrapped her in his arms and knew not when she had passed. Was this death? Her own answer seemed to come from another world:

> But angels say-and through the word
> The motion of this smile is heard,-
> 'He giveth His beloved, sleep.'

Mrs. Browning was buried in a lovely Protestant cemetery, looking toward Fiesolo. On the walls of Casa Guidi, the municipality placed a white marble slab, which in letters of gold bears the following inscription in Italian:

HERE LIVED AND DIED
Elizabeth Barrett Browning
WHO IN HER WOMAN'S HEART UNITED
THE WISDOM OF THE SAGE AND THE ELOQUENCE
OF THE POET;
WITH HER GOLDEN VERSE LINKING ITALY TO ENGLAND
GRATEFUL FLORENCE PLACED
This Memorial
A.D. 1861

One cannot mention or discuss Browning without again mentioning the love of his life, Elizabeth. Shortly after her death, the grieving poet wrote *Prospice,* a reflection of his own philosophy of this life. Death was not final; it was the summit of life, the culmination of all knowledge on this earth for the dying. He wanted to experience the full taste

Nicholas Flood Davin

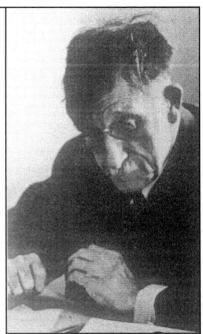

John Defoe

Thomas Roddick

Robert Service

of death and have the full understanding it would lead to a uniting with his beloved Elizabeth:

> *Fear death-to feel the fog in my throat,*
> *The mist in my face,*
> *When the snows begin, and the blasts denote*
> *I am nearing the place,*
> *The power of the night, the press of the storm,*
> *The post of the foe;*
> *Where he stands, the Arch Fear in a visible form,*
> *Yet the strong man must go:....*
> *I was ever a fighter, so-one fight more,*
> *The best and the last!*
> *I would hate that death bandaged my eyes, and forbore,*
> *No! let me taste the whole of it, fare like my peers*
> *The heroes of old....*

He concluded the poem with his own firm conviction of the immortality of the soul:

> *O thou soul of my soul! I shall clasp thee again,*
> *And with God be the rest.*

Browning lived nearly another thirty years following his wife's death. The poet, thinker, husband, lover was laid to rest in 1889 beside Tennyson in Westminister Abbey. He remains honoured for his optimistic affirmations and his belief that the universe's imperfections can be reconciled.

After being informed of a favourable review of a poetry collection, Browning uttered his last words: "How gratifying."

BRYANT AND CULLEN

One poet and two settlements named in his honour! A twenty-minute drive north from Estevan will bring you to these neighbouring communities deep in Writers Corner. Visit local cemeteries and think about life's conclusion.

WILLIAM CULLEN BRYANT (1794-1878)

Consider a response to the following: Beyond the grave there is no hell or heaven because death ends life. In other words,

> *Thine individual being, shalt thou go*
> *To mix forever with the elements,*
> *To be a brother to the insensible rock*
> *And the sluggish clod....*

Those thoughts, words and attitude are found in the poem "Thanotopsis" (literally, view of death) by W.C. Bryant. The 1817 poem's anti-Christian, stoical view of death (the poet later modified his views) made Bryant famous.

Born to a staunchly Calvinist Massachusetts family (his father was a physician of wide learning) who encouraged William to write poetry, his earliest poems reflected his family's political and religious background. His father influenced *The Embargo* by a "youth of thirteen" to be published. In later years, William wished he hadn't written the Federalist satire on Thomas Jefferson. It embarrassed the liberal adult within.

The young poet came under the influence of the British romantic poets William Wordsworth and Samuel Taylor Coleridge. Indeed, one can say that Bryant helped to introduce America to the romantic poets. His love for nature is very evident in his work. He saw the world of nature less as an escape from the evils of city life than as a positive, vital force in itself. *The Yellow Flowers, Green River, A Winter Piece*, among others, explored that idea.

In 1815 Bryant was admitted to the Massachusetts bar and he began his rather brief law practice in Great Barrington. However, he continued to write poetry and in 1821 he published his first volume, *Poems*. That year he married Frances Fairchild, his "fairest of the rural maids." He claimed that "the great spring of poetry is emotion" and that "the most beautiful poetry is that which takes the strongest hold of the feelings."

In 1826 Bryant became Assistant Editor of the liberal *New York Evening Post* and in 1829 Editor-in-chief—a post he held for a remarkable fifty years. Typical of his editorials was *The Right of Workmen to Strike* in which he wrote: "Can anything be imagined more abhorrent to every sentiment of generosity or justice, than the law which arms the rich with the legal right to fix...the ways of the poor? If this is not slavery, we have forgotten its definition." Bryant supported other liberal causes of the day including free trade, the anti-slavery movement, and the "free soil" concept. He also helped to form the new Republican Party in 1872.

In addition to his nine published volumes of poetry, he translated Homer's great works, the *Iliad* (1870) and the *Odyssey* (1872).

Clearly Bryant was one of the most popular and influential figures of mid-19th Century USA. Perhaps his famous line, "truth, crushed to earth, shall rise again," can undo lingering cynicism.

Bryant quotes of interest are:

> -*The melancholy days [of autumn] are come, the saddest of the year.*
> -*Difficulty is a nurse of greatness-a harsh nurse, who rocks her foster children roughly, but rocks them into strength and athletic proportions.*
> -*The press is good or evil according to the character of those who direct it. -It is a mill the grinds all that is put into its hopper. Fill the hopper with poisoned grain and it will grind it to meal, but there is death in the bread.*
> -*They talk of short-lived pleasures: be it so; pain dies as quickly, and lets her weary prisoner go; the fiercest agonies have the shortest reign.*
> -*Let often to these solitudes retire, and in their presence reassure my feeble virtue.*

CARLYLE

From Regina take the Trans-Canada Highway eastward to the junction of Highway #9. Turn south past Moose Mountain Park to where that highway crosses Highway #13. You've arrived at Carlyle, an important centre in Writers Corner. Anticipate that the local residents are more open and courteous than was Thomas Carlyle after whom the town supposedly was named. If you get into an argument with a woman with a Scottish accent then think of the poet's remarkable wife. Be careful.

THOMAS CARLYLE (1795-1881)

Like all great writers, Carlyle owed as much to his style as to his ideas. In a sense, he created an insistent, vital language all his own. He wrote less from his head than he did from his solar plexus and his heart. The essayist and historian, a leading figure of the Victorian era, was born in Dumfrieshire, Scotland.

The son of a small farmer and mason, Carlyle was raised in a strict Calvinist home. He later rejected Calvinism but he never escaped its harshness, integrity, respect for authority, and worship of hard work. From 1809 to 1814 he attended Edinburgh University. He walked one hundred miles to enter that institution but left without taking a degree. He rejected law, teaching and the ministry only to begin a long period of introspection and soul-searching.

In 1826 Carlyle married the clever, high-spirited Jane Welsh. Samuel Butler (1818-1893), a British historian and essayist, said of this marriage: "It was very good of God to let Carlyle and Mrs. Carlyle marry one another and so make two people miserable instead of four." They lived mostly on her Craigenputtock farm in Scotland where he began his monumental *Sartor Resartus,* called "a hodgepodge of autobiography and German philosophy."

Eight years later the Carlyles moved to London where he completed his famous *The French Revolution* in three volumes. It won critical acclaim.

Carlyle wrote much about heroes in history. He showed reverence for strength when it was combined with what might be called a God-given mission. He chose the Puritan Oliver Cromwell (1599-1658), Lord Protector of England after King Charles I was beheaded, as an example of an ideal man and leader. Carlyle's hatred and distrust of democracy, his praise for the "benificent whip," his adoration for "the strong man on horseback" did not lead to approval in many circles. His massive six-volume study of Prussia's Frederick II-another of his heroes-was less successful. Carlyle clearly became the archenemy of Victorian materialism.

Carlyle's vitriolic pen could hardly have endeared him to many of his contemporaries. His criticisms were poisonous as he rode off in all directions with his literary lance. Consider:

On Charles Lamb (1775-1834), British essayist and writer:

> Charles Lamb I sincerely believe to be in some considerable degree insane. A more pitiful, rickety, gasping, staggering Tomfool I do not know. Poor Lamb! Poor England! When such a despicable abortion is named genius.

Carlyle allowed his contempt to include all Britons. In response to an inquiry about the population of Britain, he responded, "Thirty million-all fools."

The cantankerous Carlyle lashed out at Prime Minister Disraeli: "How long will John Bull allow this absurd monkey to dance on his chest?" And this clever Scot, afflicted by chronic dyspepsia, had little time for many of his fellow writers. After reading a biography of John Keats, Carlyle wrote: "Fricassee of dead dog...the kind of man that Keats was gets more horrible to me {and}...such a soul...was a chosen vessel of hell."

Continuing to lash out in all directions, Carlyle pegged Shelley as "…a poor creature…poor soul, he has always seemed to me an extremely weak creature; a poor, thin, spasmodic, hectic shrill, shrieky, has too much of a ghost."

Clearly, Carlyle's rebukes stung: "At bottom (Thomas Bablington) Macaulay is but a poor creature with his dictionary literature and erudition, his saloon arrogance. He has no vision in him. He will neither see not do any great thing." Carlyle added: "Macaulay is well for a while, but one wouldn't live under Niagara."

The sarcastic writer who claimed that "France was long a despotism tempered by epigrams" could add this about Napoleon III: "His mind was a kind of extinct sulphur-pit."

Fellow writer Swinburne deplored "the immaculate Calvinism of so fiery and so forcible a champion of slave-holding and slave torture as Mr. Carlyle." Insults flew both ways and Carlyle refused to receive Swinburne who, he observed, "was sitting in a sewer and adding to it." Carlyle usually got the last word.

Carlyle's wife, Jane Ballie Welsh (1801-1866), notable letter-writer and wit, must be mentioned here.)In a letter to Thomas she wrote: "I am not at all the sort of person you and I took me for.") Observers considered Jane to be as stubborn and prickly as Thomas. Jane was just as thin-skinned and high-spirited as her husband, and who made him one of the most fascinating, most loyal but by no means one of the most comfortable wives a man of letters ever had. As poet Alfred, Lord Tennyson said, ""Mr. and Mrs. Carlyle on the whole enjoyed life together, else they would not have chaffed one another so heartily." The brilliant couple were not always pleasing and popular, to understate the situation.

Another story involved Carlyle's plan to write the life story of Michelangelo. The great Scot, enthused about the project, added: "Mind ye, I'll no' say much about his art."

Carlyle's negative attitude and views about the human condition are expressed in his comments on the 1861-1865 Civil War in the United States: "There they are cutting each other's throats, because on half of them prefer hiring their servants for life, and the other by the hour."

Just before Jane died, Thomas, installed as rector of Edinburgh University, delivered his speech that was later published as *On the Choice of Books*. It was an immediate success.

When Jane died in 1866, it seemed that Carlyle's pen became dry and unused. Although he received homage from many great people, his remaining years were spent in bleak loneliness.

More admired than loved, Carlyle remains a major exponent of the "Great Men Make History" theory. One can conclude with a sour note from Alfred, Lord Tennyson, poet laureate: "Carlyle is a poet to whom nature has denied the faculty of verse." Let Carlyle's advice to us be the last comment here: "He that has a secret should not only hide it, but hide that he has it to hide."

These Carlyle quotes will allow the reader to pass judgement:

-Democracy is, by the nature of it, a self-cancelling business: and gives in the long run a net result of zero.
-Literary men are...a perpetual priesthood.
-Love is ever the beginning of knowledge as fire is of light.
-Silence is deep as eternity; speech is shallow as time.
-No power of genius has ever yet had the smallest success in explaining existence.
-Society is founded on hero worship.
-All work is noble; work alone is noble.
-The fearful unbelief is the unbelief in yourself.
-The world is a republic of mediocrities, and always was.

-If Jesus Christ were to come today, people would not even crucify him. -They would ask Him to dinner, and hear what He had to say, and make fun of it.
-Be not a slave of words.
-Biography is the most universally pleasant and profitable of all reading.
-A great man shows his greatness by the way he treats little men.
-History is the essence of innumerable biographies.
-The greatest of all faults...is to be conscious of none.

COWPER

Cowper is in good company in Writers Corner. Have a picnic and tour the historic Cannington Manor a short drive north east of Carlyle. Just a nine iron away is the community of Cowper, no longer on the map but there in heart and soul. If you get lost, remember what the poet said: "God moves in a mysterious way...."

WILLIAM COWPER (1731-1800)

This English poet had a pitiful life-story. At age six he lost his mother. At school he was bullied, browbeaten and miserably unhappy. His later law studies and government service did not remove the gloom from his life: At age thirty-five he suffered the first of several lapses into insanity. He attempted suicide and was then confined to an asylum for eighteen months, troubled by religious doubts and fears. Cowper's religious melancholia was tied to the belief that he was irrevocably damned. He had a tragic sense of life and its destiny. For him, there was a fellowship with all things doomed to death. That fellowship led to his affection for mankind, for nature's plants, animals and birds. Cowper's humility and tenderness surely appeals to people who consider their lives to be beautiful but brief, tragic yet mysterious. His poems, letters and especially his hymns continue to impress. *The Poplar Trees*, among others, brought a new directness to 18th Century poetry.

Of the seven hymns examined, three verses seem to express Cowper's message best:

> *God moves in a mysterious way*
> *His wonders to perform;*
> *He plants His footsteps in the sea,*
> *And rides upon the storm.*
>
> *His purposes will ripen fast,*
> *Unfolding every hour;*
> *The bud may have a bitter taste,*
> *But sweet will be the flower.*
>
> *Blind unbelief is sure to err,*
> *And scan His work in vein;*
> *God is His own interpreter,*
> *And He will make it plain.*

In 1785 the sensitive but morbid Cowper produced a blank-verse poem running to six books in which he discussed many diverse themes.

His hymns are true lyrics in that they are the expression of the poet's religious feelings and have become part of the folk heritage of protestants everywhere.

Writer Charles Lamb wrote: "...I would not call that man my friend who should be offended with 'the divine chit-chat of Cowper.'"

One of Cowper's shorter poems, *The Solitude of Alexander Selkirk*, won considerable fame partly because of its connection with Defoe's *Robinson Crusoe.* The story of the gentle, devout, reclusive Cowper would make a fine movie. Like many people, he wins our love rather than our admiration. He kept his pervasive humour in spite of his difficulties.

The following are examples of Cowper's thoughts and quotes. He was considered the most popular poet of his generation and the best of the English letter-writers:

*Happy the man who sees God employed
In all the good and ill that checker life.*

*I had much rather be myself the slave
And wear the bonds, than fasten them on him.*

*He that has seen both sides of fifty has lived to little
purpose if he has not
other views of the world than he had when he was much
younger.*

*There is a pleasure annexed to the communication of
one's ideas, whether by word of mouth or by letter,
which nothing earthly can supply the place of.*

*Even let the unknown to-morrow
Bring with it what it may.*

*O rend of heavens, come quickly down,
And make a thousand hearts thine own.*

*'Tis universal soldiership has stabbed
The heart of merit in the meaner class.*

*Tobacco was not known in the golden age. So much
worse for the golden age.*

Variety's the spice of life, that gives it all its flavour.

Certainly Cowper had suicidal tendencies. He felt pressured when he faced a legal examination for a government post. The day before the scheduled examination, he tried to poison himself, stab himself, and hang himself. He then felt he was forever damned for committing that unpardonable sin. He tried to hang himself in 1773 and again in 1787. Three years later he died from natural causes.

Cowper deserves more attention. Here we can examine some more of Cowper's thoughts:

*-Let my ambition then excuse
My disobedience now.
-Rome shall perish-write that word
In the blood that she has spilt.
-Truth is the golden girdle of the world.*

-Grief is itself a medicine.
-He found it inconvenient to be poor.
-But strive to be a man before your mother.
-But still remember, if you mean to please,

To press your point with modesty and ease.
-A fine puss-gentleman that's all perfume.
-A poet does not work by square or line.
-Some people are more nice than wise.
-All Satan trembles, when he sees
The weakest saint upon his knees.
-Pleasure is labour too, and tires as much.
-Riches have wings.
-Our severest winter, commonly called spring.

COXBY

Near the junction of the North and South Saskatchewan Rivers, a few miles south-east of Prince Albert, you will visit the area named for its earlier post office, Coxby. The settlement was named in honour of Palmer Cox and his Granby birthplace.

PALMER COX (1840-1924)

On the man's tombstone you'll read:

IN CREATING THE BROWNIES
HE BESTOWED A PRICELESS
HERITAGE ON CHILDHOOD

The grave is that of Palmer Cox, illustrator and writer of the Brownie stories.

Cox was born in Granby, Quebec, an area populated by Scottish folk who would later influence his thought and stories. Young Palmer loved drawing even as a small child.

After his 1858 graduation from Granby Academy, he worked as a woodwork finisher on railroad cars. Then Palmer and his brother became barn framers in Ontario. Some accounts suggest that he drew pictures of many of those buildings.

Palmer loved to walk. On foot he crossed the Panama isthmus before taking a boat to Oakland, California where he became an American citizen. He worked as a builder of railroad cars and steamboats. Years later he moved to San Francisco where his serious writing career began. There he wrote periodicals and in 1874 he published his first book, *Squibs of California, or Everyday Life*, a five-hundred page effort containing sketches, poems and stories.

The following year he moved to New York to enhance his literary career. There he became the head artist for *Uncle Sam: The American Journal of Wit and Humor*. That success was followed by his verses and illustrations published in *Wide Awake*, *Harper's Young People* and *St. Nickolas*-all with children's interests in mind.

In 1883 *The Brownie's Ride* appeared in *St. Nickolas*. In all, twenty-four Brownie stories appeared before 1887. In 1890, a second series of twelve *St. Nickolas* stories were combined with a dozen others to form *Another Brownie Book*. Cox also wrote for the *Ladies Home Journal*. He continued writing children's stories that were light hearted and fun. Twelve Brownie books were eventually published.

Cox longed to return to the place of his birth so in 1905 he moved back to Granby where he planned his handsome turreted house-called Brownie Castle.

Tens of thousands of children have enjoyed Palmer Cox's drawings and stories. His characters were chosen by George Eastman for his Brownie line of Kodak cameras. The Brownies went on to adorn trading cards, dolls, children's games and other items.

The pen of Palmer Cox, illustrator and writer, brought smiles to many people.

CRICHTON

Drive west on Highway #1, wave to Swift Current, and then turn south on Highway #4 to Cadillac. Turn a little west to Admiral. Wait: You missed the community, an admirable community, called Crichton. By the way, nearby Admiral (a corruption of admirable) is also named after Crichton.

JAMES CRICHTON (1560-1582)

James "the Admirable" Crichton, called "a model of a cultured Scottish gentleman," led a short but colourful life as an adventurer, soldier, poet, swordsman, linguist, debater and scholar.

The son of the Scottish Lord Advocate, he was born in Clung, Perthshire, and educated at St. Andrews and the College de Navarre in Paris. He spent at least two years in the French army, delivered a Latin oration to the Genoa senate (1579) and took part in a great scholastic disputation in Venice the following year. In Italy he was introduced to many of the humanist philosophers and thinkers.

Some sources claim that Crichton mastered twelve languages.

The young man served the Duke of Mantua but that led to tragedy. Most of the facts have been lost but it seems that the Duke's son killed Crichton during a heated brawl.

Crichton's career was recounted by Sir Thomas Urquhart's *The Discovery of a Most Exquisite Jewel* (1652), and later was the subject of an historical novel by William H. Ainsworth (1805-1882). However, it was Sir James Barrie's 1902 play, *The Admirable Crichton*, which made the name famous. The play concerns a polymath manservant cast away with his employers on a desert island. There the subject became the perfect butler. So thanks to Barrie (1869-1937) Crichton has become synonymous with all-round talents and the ideal man.

Barrie, born in the Scottish village Kirrienmuir, was educated at Dumfries Academy and Edinburgh University. The smallish Barrie worked as a journalist in Nottingham before becoming a permanent resident in London. His heart remained in Scotland. He was deeply influenced by his mother who was immortalized in his delightful biography *Margaret Ogilvy*. The mother can be recognized over and over in Barrie's plays and novels.

Today, of course, *Peter Pan*, in print and film, has become Barrie's best known creation-among many others. The novelist, essayist, public speaker and dramatist filled his roles with distinction. A knighthood resulted.

The whimsical feature of his writing remains popular. When children tried "to fly" like Peter Pan some were badly hurt. So Barrie added a feature to the play: Children could fly only if angel dust were sprinkled on them.

Barrie valued his privacy. An obnoxious reporter came to the writer's door and said, "Sir James Barrie, I presume?" "You do," said Barrie, and slammed the door.

When the witty Barrie once dined with vegetarian George Bernard Shaw, Barrie looked at the mixture of greens and a variety of salad oils. "Tell me one thing Shaw," said Barrie, "have you eaten that or are you going to?" Humorous or disgusting?

It appears that without Barrie's reputation and hard work, Crichton would be more of a footnote in history than a well-known persona of the literary-stage-film world.

Some of Sir James Barrie's quotes serve as items of interest:

-Every time a child says "I don't believe in fairies" There is a little fairy somewhere that falls down dead.
-I do loathe explanations.
-Courage is the thing. All goes if courage fails.
-To die will be an awfully big adventure.
-There are few more impressive sights in the world than a Scotsman on the make.
-His lordship may compel us to be equal upstairs but there will never be equality in the servant's hall.
-When the first baby laughed for the first time, the laugh broke into a thousand pieces and they all went skipping about, and that was the beginning of fairies.
-That is ever the way: 'Tis all jealousy to the bride and good wishes to the corpse.
-For several days after my first book was published I carried it about in my pocket, and took surreptitious peeps at it to make sure the ink had not faded.
-I know I'm not clever but I'm always right.
-I am not young enough to know everything.
-Life is a long lesson in humility.

CUDWORTH

Enjoy your stay in Cudworth, a one-hour drive south of Prince Albert on Highway #2.

Determine how many of the locals agree with the thoughts of the 17th Century English philosopher, Ralph Cudworth, after whom the town was named.

RALPH CUDWORTH (1617-1688)

Born at Allen Somerset, Cudworth was privately educated by his step-father, Dr. Stoughton, after the youngster in 1624 lost his father, Rector and fellow of Emmanuel College, Cambridge. The father had also been Chaplain to King James.

At Cambridge University, Ralph Cudworth was greatly influenced by Benjamin Whichcote. There, for his Divinity Degree, Cudworth defended against Calvinism, Whichcote's thesis that good and evil are "eternal, immutable, and founded on reason." Both men believed that Christianity is essentially a way of life and that people should be free to choose the form of ritual and methods of church government which suit their individual temperament. For Cudworth, free will is not a form of sin.

For much of his life, this leading systemic philosopher of the Cambridge Platonists was under a cloud because of his notorious sympathy with nonconformity. He supported Cromwell's Commonwealth (after King Charles I was found guilty of treason and beheaded in 1649) as the only hope for the wider toleration. The philosopher of Hebrew, however, was concerned about the rigidity he found in Puritan thought and action. He seriously considered the "correctness" of atheism. His contemporary, the English poet-critic-dramatist John Dryden (1631-1700) responded: "[Cudworth has] such strong objections against the being of a God and Providence than many think he has not answered them." Cudworth believed that "things are what they are, not by [or] will but by Nature. Nothing can make anything evil or good which is not made so by nature."

When the monarchy was restored, it was welcomed by the eloquent Cudworth.

Serious readers can spend long months exploring the depths of Cudworth's thinking. Two examples are:

> -Sanctified afflictions are like so many artificers working on a pious man's crown to make it more bright and massive.
> -Truth and love are two of the most powerful things in the world; and when they both go together they cannot easily be withstood.

CULLEN
(SEE BRYANT AND CULLEN)

CURZON

You might say that the railroad wiped out the rural post office called Curzon near present day Allan. Take the Yellowhead Highway (#16) east from Saskatoon. In a short time turn south on #397.

Of course, that post office is long gone. So is the kind of person after whom it was named.

Perhaps you know of other "superior" individuals, voluble, eager for esteem, and primed with ambition.

GEORGE NATHANIEL CURZON (1859-1925)

Family and educational connections helped this man reach for the top! His keen intelligence and hard work also were important reasons for his success. You might say that Curzon's aristocratic bearing and appearance also added to his belief that he was a "natural", a born leader, a superior individual.

Curzon, born at Kedleston Hall, Derbyshire, learned early the importance of discipline. His strict governess and private schoolmaster made the boy pay attention, have good manners, concise speech, fine appearance and clothing, and the difficult-to-define "class".

The boy excelled. He expected that and so did his family. His boyhood was not especially happy because of the demands and expectations he experienced. At the famous Eton school he was a leader and exceptional student from 1872 to 1878. He expressed disappointment that he did not receive every possible honour during his attendance at Balliol College, Oxford from 1878 to 1882. However, he had learned that it was important for him to be in the centre of every situation.

After Oxford, Curzon travelled widely in the Mediterranean area while writing articles on the issues of the day. In 1885 Prime Minister Lord Salisbury chose him as his assistant private secretary. Two years later Curzon won his seat in the House of Commons. To 1894 he continued to write and travel extensively choosing large parts of Asia as his area of study and interest. Three fine books emerged: *Russia in Central Asia* (1889*), Persia and the Persion Question* (1892), and *Problems of the Far East* (1894).

Curzon began his government service in 1891 as under-secretary in the India office in Salisbury's government. By 1895 Curzon was the chief government spokesman on foreign affairs.

Curzon believed that it was proper that he was named Viceroy of India in 1898. For the next seven years he was in charge of the total British administration in India. He was especially concerned with India's frontiers and the possible threat from Russia, Afghanistan, Tibet and Persia.

In India, as elsewhere, Curzon's aloofness of demeanour, and insistence on formality and splendour gave rise to sharp criticisms and considerable dislike. However, military matters were his undoing. He and Lord Kitchener (after whom Berlin, Ontario had a name change to Kitchener), the rather popular commander-in-chief of the Indian army, quarrelled over military organization. Prime Minister Arthur Balfour then removed Curzon from his post. Curzon bounced back. In 1916 he was brought into the five-man War Cabinet of Prime Minister Lloyd George. In 1919 he was named Foreign Secretary. (In that role he presided at the 1922-1923 Lausanne Conference.) Four years later he thought he was the leading candidate for the Prime Ministership. To Curzon's surprise and deep disappointment Stanley Baldwin was chosen. Curzon commented on Baldwin: "Not even a public figure. A man of no experience. And of the utmost inexperience." After his victory, Baldwin met the defeated man and reported: "I met Curzon in Downing Street, from whom I got the sort of greeting a corpse would give to an undertaker." Curzon, however, continued his public service to his death.

The clever, dedicated, hard-working George Nathaniel Curzon, I[st] Marquis Curzon of Kedleston, was one of those imperialists who determined that "the sun never set on the British Empire."

However, there are stories that are hardly flattering to Curzon. When he happened to see some soldiers bathing during the First World War, he said: "I never knew the lower classes had such white skins." Another story involves Curzon's first trip by public bus: "I hailed one at the bottom of Whitehall and told the man to take me to Carlton House Terrace. But the fellow refused." A third rather doubtful story involves Curzon's instructions to his second wife regarding love-making: "Ladies never move."

Humourist Max Beerbohm referred to Curzon as "Britannia's butler." Curzon's stiff-necked attitudes and self-importance were noted years earlier in this university comment. The rhyme:

> *My name is George Nathaniel Curzon,*
> *I am a most superior person.*
> *My cheek is pink, my hair is sleek,*
> *I dine at Blenheim once a week.*

Years later at Oxford University where in 1922 Queen Mary was awarded an honorary degree, Vice-Chancellor Curzon was asked to approve the menu for the day's luncheon. His comment: "Gentlemen do not take soup at luncheon."

This aristocrat was a different sort of fellow. The epitaph on his tomb includes the following: *In diverse offices and in many lands as explorer, writer, administrator and ruler of men, he sought to serve his country and add honour to an ancient name.*

DAFOE

Take the Yellowhead Route (#16) east from Saskatoon and picnic at Big Quill Lake. You'll spot Dafoe, named for one of the most influential "pen holders" in Saskatchewan history.

Now there's a community which might well attach a printing press to a high pedestal, don't you think?

JOHN WESLEY DAFOE (1866-1944)

"The huge, roughset figure, the shaggy head of reddish hair, the carved- stone face" described J.W. Dafoe, "the oracle of Winnipeg" who was "the greatest Canadian of his time [and who] did a large part of Canada's thinking" for nearly fifty years. "The ubiquitous reporter and wisest counsellor {and} ablest political thinker" was the voice and heart of the Liberal Party. Those observations were made by the distinguished journalist-author, Bruce Hutchison.

Born in the Ottawa Valley bush country, Dafoe was raised on Shakespeare, the Bible and the *Toronto Globe*. Later he became a reporter in Montreal and then in Ottawa where he recorded some of John A. Macdonald's speeches. The young journalist later became advisor to and admirer of Prime Minister Wilfred Laurier who he described as "a man who had affinities with Machiavelli as well as Sir Galahad." As Hutchison stated, "for twenty years [Dafoe] watched over the shoulder of Mackenzie King, with a look of general approval but some scepticism." When Conservative Prime Minister Borden went to the 1919 Peace Conference he took Dafoe with him as advisor and observer. (Dafoe once said of Borden: "A Grit in disguise or [else] I'm a Tory.) Dafoe firmly believed that "the making of peace is in fact more difficult than has been the winning of the war."

As editor of the *Manitoba*, later *Winnipeg Free Press* from 1901 until his death, he became one of the most influential journalists in Canadian history. The proud Canadian was read "across the nation". Some observers considered him a lone voice against the growing power of Adolf Hitler. Dafoe was angered by the Munich appeasement and the way Mackenzie King initially underestimated the dictator (the Prime Minister called Hitler "a simple sort of peasant") before WW II. After Munich, the irrepressible Dafoe took his stubby pencil and scribbled his most famous editorial, headed "What's the Cheering For?" He knew it was a fake peace. He correctly claimed that Hitler would conquer Europe, threaten democracies everywhere, and drag America into war. Many people disagreed with him.

The rumpled newsman believed that "a Prime Minister under the party system as we have it in Canada is of necessity an egotist and autocrat." Dafoe continued: "If he comes to office without these characteristics his environment equips him with them as surely as a diet of royal jelly transforms a worker into a queen bee." The critic-observer added: "The ego and the country soon become interblended in his (PM) mind."The Prime Minister, according to Dafoe, is not merely the first among equals, not just the chief minister. He is the boss. He remains Prime Minister just as long as he wins elections.

On a 1921 voyage to the Commonwealth Conference in Australia, another journalist asked Dafoe (raised in a Conservative family) why he was such a dyed-in-the-wool Grit (Liberal). "Very simple," he responded, "I simply think of all the sons-of-bitches in the Tory Party, and then I think of all the sons-of-bitches in the Liberal Party, and I can't help coming to the conclusion that there are more sons-of-bitches in the Tory Party." Strong words from a tea totaller!

As a man of the political centre, he distrusted the extremes of the left and the right. He wrote several books including *Laurier: A Study in Canadian Politics* and *Canada: An American Nation*. "More than any country in the world," he wrote, "Canada is the result of political, not economic forces."

It remains difficult to name a Canadian political writer who has had more influence than John Wesley Dafoe. A memorable quote from Dafoe: "There are only two kinds of government-the scarcely tolerable and the absolutely unbearable." His pen was sharp: "Politics in its more primitive and vigorous manifestations is not a game of sport, but a form of civil war, with only lethal weapons barred."

The man had his moments of self-deprecation and quiet humour. When he was offered a title he responded: "How could I accept a knighthood? Good heavens! I shovel off my own sidewalk and stoke my own furnace." He had other moments when he wrote:

-Man must know, if he has any capacity for reason, that modern war doesn't come to an end...and it sets going a process of destruction that goes on tear after year in widening circles of damage and violence.
-Men may fail to be heroes to their valets but they are more successful with their biographers.-The vast repository (Hansard) of talk.

-It is no part of a newspaper's function to defend a corporation: it is always able to defend itself.
-The British Empire is a partnership of nations of equal status united in a partnership of consent.-There is no mania quite so self-revealing as that of Jew-baiting.
-Memory is one of the least reliable manifestations of the mind; it is the handmaid of will and desire.
-Unless we can trade with the outside world our condition must be one of stagnation....

J.W. Dafoe: One of Canada's genuine characters!

DANA

Take highway #5 east from Saskatoon to the junction of #2 Highway. Travel north twenty minutes or so and in the east you will spot Dana.

Now, aren't you glad you studied all that science when you were in school?

Surely the scientist who "lent" his name to the community would be pleased that nearby a RCAF radar station was established.

JAMES DWIGHT DANA (1813-1895)

Here is a top-notch zoologist and geologist, an author of standard works on geology, minerology, and studies of corals, crustaceans, and volcanoes. James was born and raised in Utica, New York where he attended Charles Bartlett's academy. There he consistently displayed his studious disposition and love for the sciences.

Before graduation, he left Yale University to become an instructor in the navy which involved a cruise to the Mediterranean Sea. Soon the American exploring expedition to the South Seas appointed the young man mineralogist and geologist. The ship was later wrecked near the mouth of the Columbia River so Dana and party travelled overland to San Francisco where they joined a companion ship, the *Vincennes.* The ship returned in 1842 to New York by way of the Cape of Good Hope. For many years Dana's pen was very busy writing his reports on his findings. Earlier he had succeeded his mentor Benjamin Gilliman as editor of *The American Journal of Science.* Dana settled in as professor at Yale-a position he held for over forty years. There he wrote more and more about his discoveries made in the South Seas.

Dana's *System of Minerology* (1837), *A Manual of Geology* (1862) and *Textbook of Geology* became a standard works. Edition followed edition. After a second visit to the Hawaiian Islands he wrote his *Characteristics of Volcanoes.*

D'ARCY and McGEE

The busy Highway #7 between Rosetown and Kindersley will allow you stops at McGee and D'Arcy, bordering on the Bad Hills. Both settlements were named after D'Arcy McGee, victim of one of Canada's few political assassinations.

D'ARCY McGEE (1825-1868)

The hanging went smoothly. The hangman, noose and trap door worked flawlessly. Before a large crowd, young Patrick James Whelan plunged to his death. It was Canada's last public execution. The Irish-born tailor and alleged Fenian was arrested within hours of the assassination on April 7th, 1868 of the poet-journalist-public speaker-historian-politician D'Arcy McGee, shot dead at his door on Sparks Street in Ottawa. Even while standing on the scaffold, Whelan proclaimed his innocence. There were and are serious doubts that he was, in fact, the assassin.

It seems clear that the Irish-born McGee, dreamer and man-of-action, was the most eloquent of the Fathers of

Confederation, Most of his short life (he was shot a week before his 43rd birthday) was spent outside Canada. He emigrated from Ireland at age seventeen and in two years he was the editor of the *Boston Pilot*. In 1845, he returned to Ireland where he was an editor for the nationalist *Nation*. After taking part in the 1848 rebellion, he fled to USA where for ten years he edited various newspapers through which he tried to improve the welfare of hundreds of thousands of Irish who had escaped from Ireland's horrid famine.

In 1857 McGee moved to Montreal at the request of the Irish community. He started his newspaper, *New Era*, which called for a "new nationality". His writings advocated a settlement of Canada's west, the building of a transcontinental railway, protective tariffs, and the development of a made-in-Canada literature.

McGee was elected to the Legislative Assembly of the Province of Canada in 1858. He later joined with John A. Macdonald and Etienne Cartier. He was in the "Great Coalition" and he attended the Charlottown and Quebec Conferences that led up to Confederation.(There were thirty six individuals who were fathers of Confederation. A core group, known as "the Big Seven" included George Brown, George E. Cartier, Alexander T. Galt, John A. Macdonald, Samuel L. Tilley, Charles Tupper and D'Arcy McGee.) He strongly opposed the Fenians, and their threat to Canada.

Perhaps some Canadians forget McGee's contribution to our nation's poetry:

> *He told them of the river, whose might current gave*
> *Its freshness for a hundred leagues to ocean's briny*
> *way.*
> *He told them of the glorious scene presented to his*
> *sight,*
> *What time he reared the cross and crown on*
> *Hochelaga's,*
> *And of the fortress cliff that keeps of Canada the key,*
> *And they welcomed back Jacques Cartier from his*
> *perilous sea.*

His poetry, his histories of Ireland, his speeches, his editorials all illustrate his marvellous use of words. One is impressed with what one of his boyhood teachers said of him. "[He is] truthful, upright, high-principled, gentle and amiable." Perhaps Isabel Shelton said it best about the martyred McGee:

> *"[He is] one who breathed into our Dominion the spirit of a proud self-reliance, and first taught Canadians to respect themselves. Was it a wonder that a cry of agony rang throughout the land when murder, foul and most unnatural, drank the life-blood of Thomas D'Arcy McGee?"*

It is likely that McGee's "call for Canadianism" is his greatest legacy. Many readers of today might agree with his powerful prose from the Confederation Debates of February 9th, 1865:

> *...These are frightful figures {referring to the numbers of soldiers and guns possessed by the United States} for the capacity of destruction they represent, for the heaps of carnage that they represent, for the quantity of human blood spilt they represent, for the lust of conquest that they represent, for the arrest of the onward progress of civilization that they represent....*

> *...They[(the United States] coveted Florida, and seized it; they coveted Louisiana, and purchased it; they coveted Texas and stole it; and then they picked a quarrel with Mexico, which ended by their getting California...had we not the strong arm of England over us, we would not now have had a separate existence....*

In McGee's case, was the pen mightier than the sword? A messenger informed Prime Minister John A. Macdonald that his colleague McGee had been shot dead. Late at night the Prime Minister hastened to McGee's body, still lying in the street. He saw McGee's head wound, his hat, and his half-smoked cigar. Macdonald helped to lift the dead man and carry him to a nearby house. That afternoon in the House of Commons, the exhausted Prime Minister listened to the speeches honouring McGee. The practical leader then rose to propose an annual annuity for McGee's widow, and a modest settlement for McGee's daughters.

Another Macdonald-McGee story places the two friends in close conversation. The drunk Prime Minister said: "Look here McGee, two drunkards is too much for any government and one of us has to stop, so I suggest you quit."

However, it was a very serious, sober McGee who penned these mighty words in 1862:

> *All we have to do is, each for himself, to keep down dissentions which can only weaken, impoverish and keep back the country, each for himself do all he can to increase its wealth, its strength and its reputation; each for himself-you, and you, gentlemen, all of us. {We must} welcome every talent, to hail every invention, to cherish every gem of art, to foster every gleam of authorship, to honour every acquirement and every gift, to lift ourselves to the level of our destinies, to rise above the low limitations and narrow circumscriptions, to cultivate that true catholicity of spirit which embraces all creeds, all classes and all races. In order to make of our boundless province, so rich in known and unknown resources, a great new Northern nation.*

Do not McGee's words need to be heard and read today? Read on:

> *-I do not believe it is our destiny to be engulfed into a Republican union.... -What really keeps nations intact and apart? – a principle.*
>
> *-...no man need blush at forty for the follies of one-and-twenty, unless, indeed, he still perseveres in them.*
>
> *-That shot fired at Fort Sumter...told the people of Canada...to sleep no more except on their arms. (In reference to the start of the American Civil War, 1861-1865)*
>
> *-We [Canadians] have no aristocracy but of virtue and talent....*

-Who will oppose-who are now opposed to our [Canadian] union? Only those who have a vested interest in their own insignificance.

-Never yet did the assassin's knife reach the core of a cause or the heart of a principle. (Reference to the murder of Abraham Lincoln)

-What me love best they defend best; what they truly believe in, for that they will bravely die.

-I believe the existence of a recognized literary class will by and by be felt as a state and social necessity.

-We know not His face, we know not His place, but His presence and power we know.

-Geographically we [Canadians] are bound up beyond the power of extinction. ...origin and language are barriers stronger to divide men in this world than is religion to unite them.

It was Joseph Howe, though not agreeing with his politics, who described McGee as "a man of genius-an elegant writer, an eloquent speaker, and a pleasant fellow over a bottle of wine."

DAVIN

A few minutes east of Regina and part of Writers Corner is Davin, named for one of Canada's most colourful characters. Determine how many locals know the early history of the newspaper they read over their morning coffee. Do they know the "connection" between their community and the nearby Richardson district?

NICHOLAS FLOOD DAVIN (1843-1901)

The flamboyant Irish-born Davin, journalist-lawyer-politician-writer, cut a wide swath in what is now Saskatchewan. Now there was a character!

He was educated at Queen's College, Cork and the University of London. Davin moved to Canada in 1872 and worked in Toronto as a reporter before being called to the

Ontario bar in 1874. The highlight of his brief legal career was when he defended the murderer of George Brown, famed Canadian politician-journalist.

The man who came to be widely known as the "Voice of the North-West" moved to Regina where in 1883 he established and edited the *Regina Leader*, the first newspaper of the Assiniboia district. His paper carried detailed reports of the 1885 trial of Louis Riel.

The resourceful and brilliant journalist donned clerical garb, a false beard, large hat and a very large crucifix and, in French, talked his way into the prison which held the condemned Metis leader. On the eve of Riel's execution Davin recorded the condemned man's last thoughts and wishes which were printed on execution day, November 16th, 1885.

Two year later, the spell-binding speaker was elected Conservative member of Parliament for West Assiniboia, and held that seat until his defeat in 1900. Four years earlier, in 1896, he won the election by one vote-cast by the returning officer who broke the tie. Davin, a visionary-dreamer, perhaps prematurely strove for provincial status for the NWT. He favoured the creation of one province to cover the whole area involved. Davin, parliamentarian, worked hard for the improvement of the living conditions faced by new settlers. On frequent occasions he wrote and spoke in favour of female suffrage.

Davin had the energy and time to write a little poetry and an unpublished novel. Years earlier he wrote:

> *As for me, I'm time-weary,*
> *I await my release.*
> *Give to others the struggle,*
> *Grant me the peace;*
> *And what peace like the peace*
> *Which death offers the brave?*
> *What rest like the rest*
> *Which we find in the grave?*

When Nicholas Flood Davin said his farewells after his 1900 election defeat few people realized how hurt and disappointed he was. A few months later, in Winnipeg, his life was ended by a self-inflicted bullet wound.

What a movie could be made! Call it after Davin's nickname, *"The Bald Eagle of the Plains"* His own words say much:

-Happy self-conjurers, deceived, we win
Delight and ruled by fancy live in dreams.
-And speaking of quotation, what is its use? ...[It]
enables you sometimes to put into the hearer's mind
what you hardly dare, and could not, put into your own
words.
-The Cabinet of Antiques. (on the Bowell
administration, 1894-1896)
-Illusion makes the better part of life.

DILKE

Picnic at Grand View Beach on Last Mountain Lake-an hour's drive north-west of Regina. Then head west. Before your lunch settles you will be in Dilke. Where is your Union Jack?

CHARLES WENTWORTH DILKE (1843-1911)

One of Britain's greatest imperialists seemed destined for success. Young Charles at Cambridge University was president of the union, senior legalist in the law tripos, and lead boatsman (stroke) of the famed university team.

At age twenty-three, the well-connected Dilke made a voyage around the world visiting New Zealand, Australia, India, Ceylon and Egypt, among others. Those experiences left him "with a conception...of the grandeur of our race, already girding the world, which it is destined, perhaps, to overspread." Dilke described those travels in his 1868 book, *Greater Britain*.

Dilke, the imperialist and radical, was no supporter of the monarchy. As a Liberal politician and M.P. he made frequent speeches favouring republicanism. He drew the attention of Disraeli who considered him to be one of the most remarkable young men he knew. For some years Dilke was seen as the chief spokesman from the opposition desks. He loudly spoke in favour of upgrading conditions for England's workers. For those people, Dilke demanded decent housing and a minimum wage.

Sir George Trevelyan commented: "I never knew a man of his age, hardly ever a man of any age, more powerful and admired than was Dilke." Trevelyan admired the way Dilke combined his knowledge of foreign affairs, his capacity for working with people of varied views, and his radical principles.

Scandal undid Dilke's career. In 1885 he was cited as co-respondent in a divorce suit brought by a fellow M.P., Donald Crawford. Mrs. Crawford was the sister-in-law of Dilke's brother, Ashton. The case was eventually dismissed but the damage was done.

When the divorce problems arose, Dilke's fiancee, a widow, was in India. She had the courage and trust to have her engagement to Dilke announced in the *Times*. Their marriage was strong-to her death in 1904. Dilke's second wife, Emelia Francis, was a successful writer whose work on eighteenth Century French painters was much appreciated.

Sir Charles Wentworth Dilke published three books on military defence and numerous volumes on colonial questions. His *Army Reform* and his *The British Empire* (1899) were particularly successful. *The Book of the Spiritual Life* (1905) contains a fine memoir of the second Lady Dilke. A busy pen.

Dilke's knowledge of foreign affairs and his ability as a critic-writer on military questions, and his potential as a future Liberal leader all suggested that he would become a most important and useful diplomat for his country. It didn't happen!

C.W. Dilke: A man of near-greatness (?)

DRAKE

Have your salty swim and float at Manitou Lake near Watrous and then head east to Drake. The mallard drake doesn't like salt water so shower before you arrive, please.

Watch for a bearded pirate with pistols and a sharp sword.

FRANCIS DRAKE (1540(?)-1596)

Here was the Englishman who circumnavigated the world in 1577-80, the naval warrior who led the English 1588 victory over the Spanish Armada (and "singed the King of Spain's beard"), the sailor who plundered and stole for Queen Elizabeth who knighted him on board the *Golden Hind,* the slaver who, with his relative John Hawkins, earlier brought slaves to the "New World," the explorer who claimed Nova Albion (New England) and California for his Queen, a fighter distrusted and disliked by some English but hated by countless Portuguese and Spanish, and the daring seafarer who brought stolen silver, spices and treasures home to England. Arise Sir Francis!

It was the same Tavistock-born Protestant Drake who twice-daily held religious services on board ship. He was the sea captain who captured the excellent and experienced Portuguese pilot-captain Nuno da Silva only to use the man to serve England's cause. Drake was a life-long student of the use of the compass, astrolabe, the cross-staff and the quadrant-all tools of his trade. He mastered those tools as a practical navigator and practical astronomer. He was an expert with the Pole-Star (Polaris or North Star) readings and solar sightings. He used his astronomical tables and navigational charts to great advantage. (Sailors of the time had no way of determining longitude so maps were crucial. "Dead reckoning," Drake's great ability, was necessary, as well.) Drake kept his logs and journals carefully during his 65,000 kilometre journey.

Should this man of action be considered "a person of the pen" to be included with others in this book? Answer: A hesitant "yes". His knowledge, intelligence, daring and determination allowed him to "put it all together" with pen (quill) and ink. The resulting maps and charts led to many further discoveries.

This man of action, after suffering from severe dysentery for some time, died off the coast of Panama. Drake's body was placed in a lead casket and he was slipped overboard to the sea that he travelled, explored and loved. The twice-married mariner left no children to continue his endeavours on behalf of the Queen.

Recent research suggests that Drake reached Vancouver Island and the Queen Charlotte Islands. What the pirate-explorer (Drake) named Nova Albion might really have been Comox on Vancouver Island.

DUFF

A few minutes south-west of Melville is Duff. Avoid arguments with the locals. They might well have the law on their side. Ask if they differentiate between justice and legality. And if so, how?

LYMAN POORE DUFF (1865-1955)

What would you say about an important and famous Canadian who never learned to drive a car let alone own one? A man who spent three months "drying out" in a hospital before returning to his lofty position? An oft-bankrupt man who failed to handle adequately his own finances but gave one-hundred dollar tips? An individual who had stacks of books-books he simply forgot to pay for? An Ottawa golfer who had his name posted for non-payment of dues? A person who got physically sick when sentencing a man to death-while still believing in the correctness of capital punishment?

You would be talking about Sir Lyman Poore Duff, Chief Justice of Canada, 1933-1944.

Duff, a man of massive intellect, sterling integrity, great energy and enduring industry was one of the most distinguished judges in Canadian history. He wrote or participated in nearly two thousand lawsuits. Consider what Norman Robertson said about Duff: "The true symposiarch who, wherever he sat, was at the head of the table. We all knew that Sir Lyman was a very great man indeed...."

That same Duff rose from humble beginnings in Meaford, Ontario where his father served as a preacher. When Lyman was a small boy, the family moved to Liverpool, Nova Scotia. He attended a rough one-room school in nearby Brooklyn. Apparently it was there that he developed a life-long love for the sea. By age ten, the bright boy, encouraged by his mother, read Dickens, Shakespeare, Hansard and military history. The bookworm was pleased to do two hours of homework each night, according to some sources.

The family returned to Ontario where Duff attended a number of elementary and secondary schools. The redheaded youth then taught school before graduating at age twenty-nine from Osgoode Hall law school. He had good but not outstanding academic results.

After travels to western Canada, Duff, in 1894, settled in Victoria where he had a lucrative and busy law practice. In 1903 he was appointed to the British Columbia Supreme Court where he had a rather undistinguished career. That same year he was part of the London tribunal which settled the Alaska Panhandle Dispute. (Alaska, in 1867, had been purchased by the USA from Russia for 7.2 million dollars. The panhandle's borders were not clearly known or defined.) Canadian lawyers like Duff found that the Americans got nearly everything they wanted plus islands in the Portland Canal.)

There were a few rough days for Judge Duff. One time, after sentencing a man to prison in Nelson, the prisoner's friend nailed Duff on his head with a baseball bat. Duff has his nose broken and he received scars which he carried for the rest of his life.

At age forty-one, Duff, a staunch Liberal, became the youngest person thus far appointed to the Supreme Court of Canada. His wife, the former Elizabeth (Lizzie) Bird, a teacher six years his senior, was proud of her husband's success. (It is uncertain why she deceived her husband regarding her age.) The couple were childless. In 1914 she was even more pleased when Duff was appointed to the British Privy Council. In 1933 he was named Chief Justice of Canada's highest court. He valued his warm friendship with Prime Minister Mackenzie King, another strong Liberal.

Earlier, the famous Person's Case saw Duff rise to the occasion. In 1927 a petition was submitted by five prominent Alberta women, Nellie McClung, Irene Parlby, Emily Murphy, Louise McKinney and Henrietta Muir Edwards and was directed by the Federal Government to the Supreme Court-and the women lost on a technicality. Duff disagreed with his colleagues. On October 28th, 1929 the Judicial Committee of the Privy Council ruled that "women were persons" under the law. Murphy could become a senator.

Perhaps Duff's greatest contribution to Canadian nationhood was his 1940 decision upholding the power of the Dominion Government to abolish appeals to England's Privy Council. (The legislation, however, didn't take effect until January 1st, 1949.) Canada, thusly, had its own "final court."

Conservative Prime Minister Bennett, in 1934, named Duff to a further high honour. At his investiture in Rideau Hall, Governor General Bessborough announced that Duff was on the New Years Day Honour List and that he had become a "member of the Knights of Grand Cross of Our Most Distinguished Order of Saint Michael and Saint George." Rise, Sir Lyman!

As noted earlier, this distinguished Canadian had his foibles and troubles. After his wife died, his sister and friends helped him to moderate his drinking. Upon his retirement from the Supreme Court-after eleven years-he lived alone in a three-story house in Ottawa. The home bulged with books, some of which remained unpaid for. The old gentleman suffered kidney problems and he died peacefully at age ninety.

Some critics claim that Duff was more a technocrat than a judge with sweep and vision. Others quickly jump to his defence and maintain that he was Canada's foremost jurist. The jury is still out. But who can deny that he wielded a powerful pen?

That same writer said this about lawyers:

Every lawyer knows that no system of law worthy of the name, whether it be cast in the form of a code or not, can be a mere collection of mechanical rules. By the law, a lawyer means the law in operation, the law in action; the law as it is commonly said is a living organism, possessing like every living organism, within limits, of course, the power to adapt itself to changing circumstances.

That doesn't sound like a technocrat.

DUMAS

Some say that the settlement was named for the son. Others say that it was named for both the father and the son. (One former resident of the Dumas area reported that he would be ashamed if the name came from the elder Dumas.)

Get involved in the argument when you visit the community immediately north of Kenosee Park, a beautiful part of Writers Corner.

ALEXANDER DUMAS (1824-1895)

Alexander *fils* (son), the illegitimate son of Alexander *pere* (father), possessed a fair amount of his father's literary talent. However, it is difficult to compare the father and son. The father, proud of his African blood, was the creator of the *Count of Monte Cristo*, *The Three Musketeers*, *The Black Tulip*, among others. He was the grandson of Domingan slave named Marie Cessette Dumas. His father, a mulatto, took the name Dumas when he joined the French army.

The son is considered a founder of "the problem play"-a middle class drama treating societal problems and offering solutions to those problems. The younger Dumas' first success was the novel *The Lady in the Camillias* (1848) but he really excelled when he adapted the story into a play known in English as "Camille". (Giuseppi Verdi based his opera *La triviata* on the play. It also provided the movie star Greta Garbo with one of her most memorable roles in 1937.) The playwright-novelist son was an unhappy witness to some of his father's illicit love affairs. On another occasion the elder Dumas listened to the description of two beautiful women. One had a glorious figure and the other had a magnificent face. Dumas observed: "I would prefer to go out with the second and come home with the first."

Dumas *pere* had a succession of mistresses which included dressmaker Marie Lebay by whom he had his son Alexander in 1824. Actress Belle Krelsamer bore him his daughter Marie Alexandrine in 1831. Son Henry Bauer in 1851 and daughter Micaella Cordier in 1860 were also born out of wedlock. An aspiring writer sent his manuscript to Dumas suggesting that the two collaborate. Dumas wrote: "How dare you team together a naked horse and a contemptible ass?" The younger man replied: "How dare you call me a horse!" Even the great Dumas lost that confrontation.

The writer son used some of his plays as "sermons" on the sanctity of marriage and the family. *Le Demi-Monde*, for example, examines the threat of prostitution to the institution of marriage. His *A Prodigal Father* is his dramatic interpretation of his father's character.

Because of his plays with a moral or social theme, Alexander *fils* is considered by many as a creator of the modern comedy of manners. It was Dumas *fils* who said, "One should never take one's daughter to a theatre. Not only are plays immoral; the house itself is immoral."

Was the son the father of the man? Here are his father's quotes:

-*Cherchez la femme.*
-*All human wisdom is summed up in two words: wait and hope.*
-*My father was a Creole, his father a Negro, and his father a monkey; my family, it seems, begins where yours left off.*
-*Tous pour un, un pour tous. (All for one, one for all)*
-*All generalizations are dangerous, even this one.*
-*I prefer rogues to imbeciles, because they sometimes take a rest.*

DUMMER

Drive south from Regina on Highway #6 for an hour or so. Stop. To the west are The Dirt Hills. However, before you reach the hills you will be in the Dummer neighbourhood, named after William Dummer Powell.

Obviously you should sit on a bench: Render justice in Writers Corner.

WILLIAM DUMMER POWELL (1755-1783)

Anne Murray was in love with William Powell, a young fellow with a dubious future. Anne and her sister had been sent by their rather poor parents to their Aunt Elizabeth's home and business in Boston. There, the young English women worked in their aunt's millinery shop, positions they felt were "below their station." William, who was from a well-to-do Loyalist family, married Anne. The Powells, loyal to the crown, left for England when the American Revolution (1775-1783) threatened.

In England, William studied law at the Inns of Court. He and Anne started their family-a baby every two years or so. The war in America was going badly for the British so in 1779 William successfully applied for a judicial appointment in Quebec, and then soon moved to Montreal. For many years the Powells and their growing family (Anne had nine pregnancies) moved from post to post including Detroit, Niagara, and Massachusetts. William's acceptance of positions in the United States caused many to doubt his loyalty to Canada and the crown.

In Montreal he served as a spokesman for the Loyalists' dissatisfaction with the 1774 Quebec Act which guaranteed the French population certain language, religion and legal rights. He also lobbied unsuccessfully for an elected assembly.

After twenty-three years "on the road" the Powells settled in York (later Toronto), Upper Canada. There, William Dummer Powell was made judge of the Court of King's Bench. In 1807 he became a member of the Executive Council of Upper Canada. (Upper and Lower Canada were formed under the 1791 Constitutional Act.) The clever and hard-working Powell became speaker of the Legislative Council and Chief Justice.

Powell's professional success was not matched by his family's success and happiness. Three sons died before maturity, another son proved indolent, a fifth son suffered from acute alcoholism. Their thirty- year-old daughter drowned when her ship went down near Ireland. The other daughters, however, seemed to have happy lives.

When William died, he left a sizeable fortune to his wife and remaining children.

ELSTOW

It is a splendid story: In 1907 a railroad official was reading John Bunyan's *Pilgrim's Progress* as the train first chugged through the area. The reader loved the book so he named the settlement Elstow in honour of Bunyan's birthplace.

Take the Yellowhead (Highway #16) east from Saskatoon. Then, pilgrim, progress to Elstow, less than an hour away.

JOHN BUNYAN (1628-1688)

Although the village boy had very little formal education he had an acute sense of sinfulness and an extraordinary power of imagination, and the two, acting together, made him miserable almost to insanity. At age sixteen John, tinker or mender of kettles and pots, left his father's shop and home to join the army because he couldn't stand his step-mother. It was during his three-year military service when he came in touch with certain religious elements in the army of Puritan Oliver Cromwell (1599-1658).

Bunyan then returned to his father's Elstow home but soon he met a poor woman, and they married "without so much household stuff as a dish or a spoon." His wife, who died in 1656 leaving four children, did possess two religious books that helped to ease John's mental and spiritual torture. (He remarried three years later.) At age twenty-seven, he later claimed, he received "comfortable words" from Heaven, and his inner struggles were over.

After his conversion Bunyan became a preacher in a non-conformist (Puritan) congregation. Wherever his tinker trade took him is where he preached. He attracted large crowds in barns, meadows and street corners. In 1660 John Bunyan was charged with holding a service not in conformity with the Church of England. He refused to change so he was imprisoned for twelve years. On occasions he was let out to visit family and friends, and to address some meetings. The Restoration of Charles II had ended twenty years of comparative religious freedom.

In prison Bunyan studied the Bible and other "religious sources," preached to his fellow prisoners and their visitors, and began to write in plain but forceful English. In 1675 he was again in prison. There he wrote the first part of *Pilgrim's Progress*, his twenty-fourth book. That book was to take its place among the greatest imaginative works in the western world.

The simple, homely style of his masterpiece is derived from the speech of common folk and the vocabulary of the King James Bible. It was one of the first books printed in America, and it has gone into countless editions and translations. One might suggest it is one of the great marvels of literature that an individual with really no formal education should have been able to write so brilliantly. It is a true expression of the ideals of Christianity as understood by common men and women. Bunyan's eloquent and forceful writing has admirers to this day.

The tinker used his pen to inspire others. Do these words inspire?

-*The valley of humiliation.*
-*Then I saw that there was a way to hell, even from the gates of heaven.*
So he passed over, and all the trumpets sounded for him on the other side.
As I walked through the wilderness of this world.
-*Set your faces like flint.*
-*Hanging is too good for him, said Mr. Cruelty.*
-*A young woman, her name was Dull.*
-*Sleep is sweet to the labouring man.*
-*An ornament to her profession.*
-*...there was a very stately palace before him, the name of which was Beautiful.*
-*If all the fornicators and adulterers were hanged by the neck until they be dead, John Bunyan, the object of their envy, would be still alive and well.*
-*One leak will sink a ship, and one sin will destroy a sinner.*

Two hundred and seventy two years after Bunyan's book was published, a survey of readers taken by the Columbia University Press declared it was the most boring of all classics.

ESK
(SEE TROSSACHS, ESK and ROBSART)

FERLAND

A short distance north of Grasslands National Park and the Wood Mountain region, you will find Ferland. You will be on Highway #18, just a bit east of Mankota.

Enjoy the marvellous sky, the sunrises and sunsets of the Ferland community.

Should you brush up on your French? Or are you bilingual just as was Father Ferland?

JOHN BAPTISTE ANTOINE FERLAND (1805-1865)

Priest, professor and historian, Ferland was raised in a Quebec family that had been "converted to bilingualism." When he was eight, he and his widowed mother moved to Kingston, Upper Canada. The youth later entered the College de Nicolet where he earned a brilliant record in classical studies. At age twenty-two he was ordained as a priest. Ferland served numerous communities in Quebec. His devoted attention to typhus-stricken Irish immigrants on Grosse Ile earned him great respect.

In 1841 Abbe Ferland returned to the College de Nicolet where, for nine years, he was professor of history, literature and philosophy. Later he took on administrative work at the college as well.

During the 1850's Ferland's work as an historian took shape. He visited Canada-related archives in Europe and returned home to deliver many well-received public lectures on the history of Canada. Ferland's book, *Cours d'histoire du Canada* is really a reply to the liberal interpretation of this country's history. He perhaps underestimated any quarrels between church and state, and he stressed what he believed to have been unanimity among clergymen of his faith. He was anxious to demonstrate that the beneficent influence of clergy and Catholicism of colonial society.

Ferland was ahead of his time in other respects. While many nineteenth century observers had little good to say about Indian culture, he had a more positive view. He clearly understood why many natives felt alienated in the presence of Europeans. He claimed he could explain the Indian's relentless opposition to the white man. Ferland's natives are bloody and cruel, but, he claimed, this was "Indian politics." Their actions were as valid, he believed, as the whites' actions which led to troubled times and events.

Historian Ferland sharply condemned the earlier actions of Cartier and Champlain who, he said, had set the stage for further difficulty. He admired the Iroquois Confederacy and its similarity to the federated United States: Both were founded on the principle of the liberty of man, he claimed.

Ferland's credibility as a nineteenth century historian remains high to this day.

FLEMING

Your last stop in Saskatchewan as you travel eastward on the Trans Canada Highway is Fleming, named after a man with a fantastic career. Indeed, Sanford Fleming's impact is felt strongly today.

Enjoy your stay at Fleming. Perhaps you could suggest to its citizens that a statue or plaque should be made to honour that most remarkable Canadian. It would be a fine addition to Writers Corner.

SIR SANFORD FLEMING (1827-1915)

The truly remarkable Scot-born Fleming, distinguished writer, scientist, inventor, railway construction engineer and surveyor was the individual who successfully advocated the adoption of a standard or mean time and hourly variations from that according to established time zones. He was largely responsible for convening the 1884 Washington Conference at which the international standard time was adopted.

But the brilliant Canadian did more: He designed the first Canadian postage stamp, the threepenny beaver, issued in 1851.

In 1863, he was appointed chief surveyor of the first section of the proposed Quebec City to Halifax railway. In 1871, the gifted Fleming was named engineer of the proposed Montreal-to-the-Pacific rail route. His work included surveys on the prairies, the Yellowhead Route (the proposal was not then followed) and the Kicking Horse Pass. The strategy of railway building was employed to bring British Columbia into Confederation.

After leaving railroad work he became a consultant. He strongly advocated a telecommunications cable from Canada to Australia-successfully completed in 1902.

Fleming's vision, writing, planning and research were widely applauded. He was awarded honorary degrees from St. Andrews in Scotland, Columbia, Toronto and Queens. He was a charter member of the Royal Society of Canada (and its president in 1888-1889). Fleming was created a C.M.G. in 1877 and was knighted twenty years later. In 1879

Fleming's Three Pence Stamp
(Courtesy of Ed Stephen's Collection, Prince Albert)

he became Chancellor of Queens College at Kingston. In his inaugural address he made a strong case for placing science at the centre of university education. He considered his faith in knowledge to be rooted in his Presbyterian heritage.

Sir Sanford Fleming's strength lay in his systematic use of institutions for his causes. In today's terms, he was a "mover and shaker" of a very high order. Perhaps the word "promoter" best describes the scientist-businessman. It was through technology that he reached for national and international goals.

You can say that the man used his pen to good advantage.

FROUDE

Every area needs an historian or two. One such person lent his name to Writers Corner. Journey westward from Weyburn for half an hour or so to visit Froude. Be sure to describe carefully the surroundings and the people you meet-to match the exacting standards of J.A. Froude.

JAMES ANTHONY FROUDE (1818-1894)

The historian-churchman-editor was born in Dartington, Devon, England. He put to good use the education he received at Oxford. As an historian, he did not hesitate to let his prejudices show, praising some historical figures while condemning others in a rather unscholarly manner. However, he made history exciting to read. He maintained that historians must simply record human actions, and that history should be written as a drama. Like his friend and fellow historian, Thomas Carlyle, he gave prominence to "the great Man Theory of History." Central to his approach was his contention that the Protestant Reformation was "the root and source of the expansive force which has spread the Anglo-Saxon race over the globe."

Froud's twelve volumes covering English history from 1529 to 1588 (defeat of the Spanish Armada) have a strong anti-clerical bias. (Some of his earlier criticisms of the church were published under the pseudonym of *Zeta*.) His work displays a strong admiration for tough rulers and strong government, almost suggesting that tyranny is sometimes necessary and excusable.

The man had a great ability to describe his subjects and their surroundings. His description of Anne Boleyn's coronation procession is a good example. His graceful histories were widely popular, even though he was often careless with details, copying of manuscripts and proof-reading.

For fourteen years he served as editor of *Fraser's Magazine*. In 1892 he was appointed Regius professor of modern history at Oxford. His students warmly received the brilliant man's lectures. He taught his students and his readers much about the importance of motivation in the human condition.

Froude, using perhaps more frankness than judgement, wrote a biography of the great Thomas Carlyle who was his friend and mentor. The following Froude quotes reveal the depth of his thoughts:

-*Wild animals never kill for sport. Man is the only one to whom the torture and death of his fellow-creatures is amusing in itself.*

-*For every false word or unrighteous deed, for cruelty and oppression, for lust or vanity, the price has to be paid at last, not always by the chief offenders, but paid by some one.*

-*To deny the freedom of the will is to make morality impossible.*

-*Fear is the parent of cruelty.*

-*Experience teaches slowly, and at the cost of mistakes.*

-*Men are made by nature unequal. It is vain, therefore, to treat them as if they were equal.*

GAINSBOROUGH

Is there a place in Saskatchewan's Writers Corner for an artist? A master of light and colour?

Travel east on Highway #18 from Estevan. When you are a few brush strokes from the Manitoba border you will be in Gainsborough.

Watch for a boy dressed in blue.

THOMAS GAINSBOROUGH (1727-1788)

If for nothing else, Gainsborough will be remembered for his "Blue Boy", a haunting study of adolescence. However, that famous painting is only a fraction of the artist's creations.

Gainsborough's father, a prosperous English cloth merchant, realized that the boy had tremendous talent. At age twelve the lad was sent to London where he worked with and learned from mature painters. He likely copied and restored Dutch landscapes for dealers. At age nineteen he married the attractive Margaret Burr who, it appears, brought him a handsome yearly income.

By age twenty-one, Gainsborough was much admired as a landscape painter. His painting "The Charterhouse" showed a mature observation of reality and handling of light. His alternation between invention and observation became the basis of his artistic growth. He had opportunities to study the style and methods of the Dutch master, Anthony Vandyke. Before long he was ranked with the talented Sir Joshua Reynolds in London. He became famous for the elegance of his portraits, especially of women. Those works have a light and airy quality. Blues and greens dominate his work.

As Gainsborough's excellence increased, so did Reynold's appreciation and approval. The transition of

Gainsborough's painting to impressionistic abstraction was described by Reynolds as "chaos assuming form by a kind of magic." The artist had problems with his portrait of Sarah Siddons. At one sitting, he burst out in exasperation; "Damn your nose, madam, there's no end to it." Gainsborough painted portraits of such notables as Garrick, Chatterton, Richardson, Foote, Mrs. Siddons, and the Duchess of Devonshire. Some experts rank his "Harvest Waggon" with his "Blue Boy". He clearly excelled as a landscape painter and portrait painter. Whether the artist painted common folk or the aristocracy, there was a poetically evocative touch to his work.

Gainsborough: A master of light and colour. His last words: "We are all going to heaven and Vandyke is of the company." However, his most memorable comment was as follows: "Recollect that painting and punctuality mix like oil and vinegar, and that genius and regularity are utter enemies, and must be to the end of time."

GARRICK

Drive north-east of Prince Albert on Highway #55. Shortly past Choiceland, about half way to Nipawin you will find yourself in Garrick. Some claim Garrick was named for a corporal who lost his life in WW I. It seems more likely that the settlement was named for David Garrick, a genuine character, to be sure.

DAVID GARRICK (1717-1779)

Young David was lucky: At Edial, he had for his teacher the magnificent Samuel Johnson (1709-1784) later the author of the famous *Dictionary of the English Language* (1755) and the subject of John Boswell's famous biographical work. Garrick followed his mentor to London where the younger man set up a wine shop and later became a well known actor. In 1741, he appeared at Ipswich in

Oroonoko. That year, he solidified his reputation (many people called him an idol) in the part of Richard III. In both comic and tragic parts, Garrick was to have many triumphs on the stage- e.g. *Lear, Hamlet,* and *Abel Drugger.* His simple diction and manner swept declamatory actors from the stage. A famous Garrick quote: "Any fool can play tragedy, but comedy, sir, is a damned serious business." Consider another Garrick quote: "Corrupted freemen are the worst of slaves."

In 1747, Garrick joined the management of Drury Lane, a theatre named after the Drury family. (The building of that name, originally a cock-pit, was converted to a theatre during the reign of James I.) There, Garrick produced many of Shakespeare's dramas as well as Johnson's tragedy "Irene". Garrick was the co-author of *The Clandestine Marriage* and also wrote several farces. He believed that for a time the theatre was so "starchy and staid" that it would be appropriate to build church steeples over all of London's theatres.

David Garrick, a long time member of Dr. Johnson's famed literary circle, a man-about-London, a character who loved the limelight, had his portrait painted by three great artists-painters: Reynolds, Gainsborough, and Hogarth.

Garrick showed the great Dr. Johnson his fine house, gardens, statues, and pictures at Hampton Court. "Ah! David, David," said Johnson, "these are the things that make men's death terrible."

The wit and fellow-actor, Samuel Foote, kept a bust of Garrick on his bureau. Foote explained: "You may wonder that I should allow him so near my gold, but see-he has no hands."

Garrick, no stranger to wit, replied to a nobleman's request to run for parliament: "I had rather play the part of a great man on stage than the part of a fool in parliament." When a playwright sent Garrick a play to read and a horse to ride, that same Garrick replied: "When the one wants wits, and the other the spur, they both jog on very heavily. I must keep the horse, but I have returned you the play."

The talented and well-connected Garrick had correspondence with many distinguished individuals of his day. In 1831-1832 those letters were published. Quotes worth the read:

-*Prologues precede the piece-in mournful verse;*
  As undertakers-walk before the hearse.

-*Heaven sends us good food, but the devil sends cooks.*

-*Here lies Nolly Goldsmith, for shortness call'd Nol,*
 Who wrote like an angel, but talked like poor Poll.

-*Kitty, a fair but frozen maid,*
  Kindled a flame I still deplore.

-*Heart of oak are our ships,*
 Heart of oak are our men:
  We always are ready;
  Steady, boys, steady;
  We'll fight and we'll conquer again and again.

Garrick had a fierce wit, often cruel in its honesty. A lady had asked Garrick if one of her friends might have a part in a play. Garrick wrote his response: "If your Grace will permit me to speak my mind, I think he has the most unpromising aspect for an actor I ever saw-a small pair of unmeaning eyes stuck in a round unthinking face are not the most desirable requisites for a hero or a fine gentleman." Straight talk!

HANDEL

Leave Wilkie and head south on highway #658. Stop at Handel. Plug in your CD or tape. Turn up the volume. Lean back in your car seat, close your eyes, and be surrounded and thrilled by Handel's *The Messiah*.

GEORGE FREDERICK HANDEL (1685-1759)

The father, a barber-surgeon in Halle, Lower Saxony, wanted his son to become a lawyer. Instead, the boy turned to music. A friend smuggled a clavichord into Handel's attic where the youngster practised long and hard-and secretly. Eventually, other people, including a cathedral organist, recognized Handel's talent and potential. The organist gave him training as a composer and a performer on the oboe and violin. By age eleven, Handel had composed six trios for two oboes and bass. Before long the youth surpassed his teacher and was sent to Berlin for further training. Court officials were impressed.

After his father's death in 1697, the boy returned to Halle where he completed his "regular" schooling and added to his musical knowledge. He later took some law studies at the local university.

Handel's quarrel with a fellow-musician could have cost him his life. In the duel, the point of the opponent's sword struck his large chest button. The two young men "made up" and became friends.

In Hamburg, Handel's first opera, *Almira*, had great success. He moved to Italy for further work and study. During those three years he produced two operas, *Rodnigo* and *Agrippina* plus smaller works. In 1712, the musician-composer settled in England where his fame became even greater. He "moved" from opera to oratorio with remarkable successes. Over the years, in England, he experienced wealth then bankruptcy and back to wealth.

The practical genius, the associate of literary men and powerful politicians, was a man of high character and intelligence. In English oratorio Handel created a true art-form on the largest possible scale. However, in 1751 his sight began to trouble him and he underwent unsuccessful operations. He then was able to see only at intervals. In spite of his near blindness, he continued with his work.

Handel shut himself up for twenty-one days a n d emerged with the complete score of *Messiah.* At one of the London performances of Handel's *The Messiah* in 1743, the entire audience rose as one as the hallelujah chorus began-and stayed standing to the end. King George 11 was present and it is said that it was he who first got to his feet. Audiences in Britain and elsewhere often follow that tradition today when the famous chorus is played.

When Handel had completed composing Part 2 of *The Messiah* which includes the Hallelujah chorus, his servant found him at the table, tears streaming from his eyes. The majesty and the beauty and the power he had created had astounded him. Later he commented on the cause of that tearful moment: "I did think that I did see all heaven before me and the great God himself." It took George Bernard Shaw to disagree: "I think the Hallelujah chorus might be improved by steeping in boiling water for ten minutes or so. The great musician Joseph Hayden, after hearing the chorus, claimed that Handel "is the master of us all."

When the plans were made for Handel to direct *The Messiah* in Dublin, he requested that a male performer who could "sing at sight" be supplied. One fellow appeared but his attempts were dismal, indeed. After swearing in four or five languages, Handel cried out in broken English, "You shcauntrel, tit you not dell me dat you could sing at soit?" The poor fellow replied: "Yes, sir, and so I can, but not at first sight."

Another story involving the temperamental genius tells of the famous soprano, Francesca Cuzzoni, who refused to sing a piece he had written for her London debut. Handel picked up the woman, walked to a nearby high window, and threatened to toss her to the ground. The lady sang.

When another singer objected to Handel's accompaniment on the harpsichord the complainer said: "If you don't follow me better than that I'll jump on your harpsichord and smash it up." Handel responded quickly: "Please let me know when and I will advertise it, for more people will come to see you jump than to hear you sing."

A week before his death, Handel attended a performance of *The Messiah*. He was buried in Westminister Abbey. His genius is recognized to this day. Millions have been thrilled by his music. However, the talented Piotr Tchaikovsky said, "Handel is only fourth rate. He is not even interesting." A minority report!

What would you say to French composer Hector Berlioz who described Handel as "a tub of pork and beer"? Perhaps Berlioz had a point. Handel once ordered dinner for two. When he arrived at the tavern he said, "I am the company."

HARDY

Take Highway #6 straight south of Regina for a pleasant one-hour drive. Stop at Ceylon and turn west a jump or two. You'll be in the Hardy settlement, part of Writers Corner.

Ask the residents if they are as pessimistic as was the writer whose name adorns their community.

THOMAS HARDY (1840-1928)

The distinguished poet and novelist, son of a stone mason, was born in Dorsetshire, southern England. After leaving school early, he became a pupil of an architect and church restorer. By age twenty-five, Hardy was an accomplished architect.

From 1862 to 1867 he lived in London where he began seriously to write poetry. Indeed, until 1870 poetry was his first concern. That year he met his future wife, Emma Lavina Gifford (The meeting and its setting were poetically recreated by Hardy forty years later in his *Veteris Vestigiae Flammai-Vestiges of an old Flame*). Later, in fun, Hardy wrote that "a good wife is good, but the best wife is not so good as no wife at all." Most of his books were written in the house at Max Gate in Dorchester which he designed and built for Emma. Hardy's famous *Far From the Madding Crowd* was published in 1874, a novel whose reception encouraged him greatly. Later he published *The Return of the Native*, *Tess D'Ubervilles*, among others, all with mixed reviews.

All Hardy's writing make plain his stoical pessimism and his sense of the inevitable tragedy in human life. His 1910 *The Dynasts*, a large drama of the Napoleonic Wars written mostly in blank verse, clearly spell out Hardy's view: The struggle of man is against the force which is neutral and indifferent to his sufferings which rule his world.

It seems that Hardy's God is as indifferent as nature. God has forgotten that He ever made this world which was one of His failures. That is why He lost interest in this world. God knows nothing about values which, after all, are totally man-made. Over everything hovers the threat of war. Life is no "picnic."

Yet Hardy tells us that life must continue, we must overcome. Yes, Hardy does show some humour in the rustic characters of his novels. But don't be too taken by that small humour: The writer tells us that almost all human effort is vain because our lives are determined by fate.

You can sense Hardy's views in his *A Wife Waits*:

Will's at the dance in the Club-room below,
Where the tall liquor-cups foam;
    I on the pavement up here by the Bow,
    Wait, wait to steady him home.

Will and his partner are treading a tune,
Loving companions they be;
Willy, before we were married in June,
Said he loved no one but me;

Said he would let his old pleasures all go
Ever to live with his Dear.
Will's at the dance in the Club-room below,
Shivering I wait for him here.

Whatever Hardy might lose in grace he more than makes up in rugged power.

Hardy learned that one of his novels, *Jude the Obscure*, was burned by a Bishop. The author suggested, to the clergyman's chagrin, that "he was not able to burn me."

In the end, Hardy got what he wanted. His ashes were placed in Westminister Abbey's Poets Corner and his heart was supposedly buried in his beloved Dorset. After his death a relative reported that the writer's sister's cat got at the heart while it was on the kitchen table. Meal time for the cat. The burial of a tin, thought by the public to contain the heart, went ahead. Hardy likely would have been pleased to learn that the pallbearers at his funeral included George B. Shaw, Rudyard Kipling, A.E. Houseman-famous writers indeed. Politicians Ramsey MacDonald and Stanley Baldwin also served in that capacity.

Here are a few quotable gems from Thomas Hardy:

-Twin halves of one august event.
-A local cult called Christianity.
-He was a man who used to notice such things.
-That long drip of human tears.
-Love is lame at fifty years.
-Patiently adjust, amend, and heal.
-A nice unparticular man.
-Life's little ironies.
-A little one-eyed, blinking sort o' place.
-Good, but not religious good.

-The dull period in the life of an event is when it ceases to be news and has not begun to be history.
-Done because we are too menny. (a child's suicide note explaining why he has killed himself and two others.)
-A lover without indiscretion is no lover at all.

Read Hardy when you are in a rather sour mood. Your disposition won't improve as a result. As G.K. Chesterton, British novelist-poet-critic suggested, "Hardy became a sort of village atheist brooding and blaspheming over the village idiot."

HERSCHEL

Here is another Saskatchewan centre named for a genius.

Drive south west from Saskatoon on Highway #7 and turn north a bit at the junction of #656.

Why not make an evening of it? Enjoy the Milky Way, the stars, and the immensity of the sky. Be the astronomer you have always wanted to be. It will be helpful if you, too, are a genius.

JOHN F. W. HERSCHEL (1792-1871)

Was this man "programmed" to succeed? His father, William, was the eminent astronomer of the time and the discoverer of the planet Uranus. The younger Herschel studied mathematics at Cambridge where he graduated first in his class in 1813. His subsequent mathematical papers garnered him the Copley medal of the Royal Society. With colleagues, he also published a calculus textbook.

Herschel's interests turned to chemistry, and he also spent some years dabbling in optics, law and astronomy. In 1820 he yielded to what might be called his "birth debt"- and turned full time to astronomy. He and his father worked and studied together.

His restless intellect carried him to what is now called philosophy of science. He wrote *On the Study of Natural Philosophy* which was widely acclaimed.

In 1833 Herschel moved his family to South Africa for four years. There the southern skies became the focus of his study. He began his work with photometry, the precise measurement of stellar brightness.

Back in England the researcher received further honours at Queen Victoria's coronation. Earlier he had discovered the crucial property of the chemical that has since been used as the photographer's "hypo". At the time photography was in its infancy. However, Herschel invented methods of producing images on glass and paper rather than metal. He also introduced "positive" and "negative" in the photographic context.

The son also confirmed and extended his father's observations and cataloguing of nebular and double stars and the Milky Way. Both men concluded that the solar system as a whole moves through space.

John Herschel spent his remaining years working on the reduction, evaluation and publication of a tremendous amount of astronomical data.

John Herschel was knighted forty years before his death. He was buried in Westminister Abbey, honoured as a brilliant scientist.

Herschel quotes:

-Of all the amusements that can possibly be imagined in a hard-working man, after a day's toil...there is nothing like reading an entertaining newspaper.
-The novel, in its best form, I regard as one of the most powerful engines of civilization ever invented.

-If I were to pray for a taste which should stand me under every variety of circumstances...it would be for a taste of reading.

-Self-respect: the cornerstone of all virtue.

-The besetting evil of our age is the temptation to squander and dilute thought on a thousand different lines of inquiry.

-The grand character of truths is its capability of enduring the test of universal experience, and coming unchanged out of every possible form of fair discussion.

It anticipated that in 2007 the Herschel Space Observatory will be put into space. The work will further explore the mystery of how the stars and galaxies were formed.

HOLBEIN

Bring your brushes, paint and palette to Holbein, a few minutes drive west from Prince Albert. Paint your subject's portrait just as Hans Holbein would. You will likely become famous and rich as a result.

Holbein is one of the few Saskatchewan centres named in honour of a great artist.

HANS HOLBEIN (1497-1543)

Holbein, an outstanding artist of German Renaissance, was born to an artistic family. His father, Hans the elder, was a painter and a designer of stained glass as well as a silverpoint portraitist. Another son, Ambrosius, was well known for his portraits and book illustrations.

Hans Holbein spent many years in Basil, Switzerland, where he enjoyed the friendship and sponsorship of Disiderius Erasmus (1496-1536), Dutch humanist, catholic priest, teacher and writer. Holbein produced many portraits of Erasmus, and he illustrated the writer's famous *Praise of Folly*. The painter also spent time in England. Earlier he had married a widow who gave him four children. He left his family in Basil. In London he painted many eminent people including Sir Thomas More. In 1536 Holbein was named official painter for King Henry VIII and created many portraits of this monarch by Hans Holbein. The man's portrait work consistently showed a remarkable sensitivity of line and characterization.

The painter's art is characterized by superb technical skill, a firm grasp of form and space, a keen eye for detail, and an unfailing sense of pattern and composition. Control, precision, objectivity are words used to describe his many portraits.

Holbein should be better known for his beautiful woodcuts which include *Dance of Death* and illustrations for Martin Luther's Bible. He also made designs for stained glass and jewellery.

However, Holbein's remarkable reputation rests with his portraits. Some experts claim that his unsparingly realistic *Dead Christ* (1521) and *Madonna and Child Enthroned with two Saints* (1522) best represent Hans Holbein's genius. His work brought him both fame and fortune.

By the way, King Henry VIII found his fourth wife, Anne of Cleves, to be less attractive than her portrait by Holbein.

HUMBOLDT

Pick up your favourite scientist before heading to Humboldt east from Saskatoon on Highway #5. Kindly ask your scientist friend to outline the tremendous contributions of the individual after whom the town was named. Take a tape recorder and check his/her sources. Hard work!

BARON ALEXANDER VON HUMBOLDT (1769-1859)

Here was a bachelor, benevolent in disposition but caustic in comment, a man who was unable to handle money and debts, a world traveller and a scientist whose works impacts on us today. Alexander's father, who died early, was an officer in the Prussian army. His mother was considered a "cold and aloof" individual. Alexander highly valued the warmth and love he found in his brother's household. (The brother, Wilhelm, was Prussian Minister of Education who reformed the school system and founded the University of Berlin.)

After lengthy university study he joined the mining department of the Prussian government. He studied the magnetic qualities of rocks, and he invented a safety lamp. In June, 1799 he began his famous five year exploration involving meteorological observations and botanical research. The scientist spent those years in South America and Mexico with briefer stops in Cuba and the United States. His published *Personal Narratives* was admired by Charles Darwin. Humboldt pointed out the connection between excessive lumbering and soil erosion, studied the Inca and Aztec relics, and studied the climatic conditions required for French vines. A multidisciplined individual.

For twenty-three years Humboldt lived mainly in Paris (his mother was a French Huguenot-Protestant) where he studied and worked in the field of geomagnetism which subsequently led to the discovery of the magnetic north pole in Canada. In1727 he continued his research in Berlin before leaving for nine months of mining study in Siberia where he also recorded his geological and botanical observations.

Humboldt's *Asie Centrale*, a three volume study, appeared in Paris in 1843. His magnificent five-volume study, *Kosmos*, was published in Stuttgart from 1845 to 1862. The study of geophysics, geography, geology and meteorology were all enhanced by the efforts of this dedicated scientist and writer. Here was a man who was an honoured friend to court officials, the great writer Johann Goethe (1749-1732), and Friedrich von Schiller (1759-1805), poet, historian, philosopher.

In other words, Humboldt's genius was recognized by other people of genius. The Humboldt Glacier in Greenland and the Humboldt Current in the South Pacific were named for him.

HUME

Lunch in Weyburn and then drive east on Highway #13 for about ten minutes and you will arrive at the community of Hume, part of Writers' Corner. Feel at home in Hume.

DAVID HUME (1711-1776)

The Scottish philosopher and historian has been credited with having "the clearest head of all philosophers." Yet he is the same individual who wrote that "the worst white man is better than the best black man." He was one of those thinkers who claimed that philosophy was not the handmaid of theology.

In his *First Principles of Government* (1742) Hume expressed some surprise at the submissive nature of man:

> *Nothing appears more surprising to those who consider human affairs with a philosophical eye, than the ease with which the many are governed by the few and the implicit submission with which men resign their own sentiments and passions to those of their rulers.*

The man was also an accomplished, successful historian whose *History of England* (1754-1762) became a long time standard despite errors in fact.

His determined, thorough-going scepticism led him to state that in the mind, one finds nothing but a series of sensations and the cause-effect relation in the natural world as apparent only because two sensations were customarily joined. Rejecting the possibility of knowledge that is certain, he fell back on common sense and faith.

The purity of Hume's literary style is to be found in such essays as *Treatise of Human Nature, Essays, Moral and Political, Political Discourses* and *Philosophical Essays.*

When the Geneva-born French philosopher Jean Jacques Rousseau (1712-1778) spent part of his exile in England, Hume became his patron. The two quarrelled bitterly and became enemies.

Hume's treatise of human nature tackles major problems in human existence and perception. Some aspects of his thinking still challenge modern day philosophers, in particular his explanation of cause and effect as "constant conjunction."

The historian and philosopher enjoyed a rather handsome income from his literary works and pensions. When asked to extend his *History of England* endeavour, he replied: "Gentlemen, you do me too much honour, but I have four reasons for not writing; I am too old, too fat, too lazy and too rich." British author James Caulfield added this description of Hume: "His face was broad and flat, his mouth wide and without any other expression than that of imbecility. His eyes were vacant and spiritless, and the corpulence of his whole person was far better to communicate the idea of a turtle-eating Alderman than that of a refined philosopher."

When a friend told the sceptical Hume that he was being inconsistent by going to listen to a preacher, the great man replied, "I don't believe all he says, but *he* does, and once a week I like to hear a man who believes what he says."

While visiting Paris, the stoutly-built Hume was accosted as he entered a room. The speaker quoted from

St. John's Gospel: "Et verbum caro factum est. [And the word was made flesh]" A female admirer of Hume quickly replied: "Et verbum carum factum est. [And the word was made lovable]" Some Hume quotes to ponder:

-The Christian religion was not only at first attended by miracles, but even at this day cannot be believed by any reasonable person without. one.

-Bear-baiting was esteemed heathenist and unchristian; the sport of it, not the inhumanity, gave offence.

-Weakness, fear, melancholy, together with ignorance, are, therefore, the true sources of superstition.

-Avarice-the spur of industry....

-Be a philosopher; but amidst all your philosophy, be still a man.

-All laws being founded on rewards and punishments....

-The same motives always produce the same actions. The same events follow from the same causes.

-A wise man, therefore, proportions his belief to the evidence.

-I believe that no man ever threw away life while it was worth keeping. (From "Of Suicide")

-Beauty in things exist in the mind which contemplates them.

-In all ages of the world, priests have been enemies of liberty.

IBSEN

An important name from the world of literature graces the settlement called Ibsen, very much a part of Writers Corner.

Drive south-east on Highway #39 from Moose Jaw toward Weyburn. Pass through Milestone and Lang-and then you will have arrived.

Hilsen fra Norge!

HENRIK IBSEN (1828-*1906*)

Ibsen, "the Colossus of the North" and the so-called father of modern drama, was a rebel all his life. The recurrent word in Ibsen's lexicon was "liberty," and his constant clamour was for freedom. Making supreme sacrifices for one's beliefs was for him the acid test of sincerity. (Now there's a character worth of further investigation!)

Ibsen was born in Skein, Norway, a small town one hundred miles south of the capital Christiana (now Oslo). He was two-thirds Norwegian, one-sixth Danish with a little Scot and German added. Nevertheless, the playwright later asserted that he had no Norwegian blood. Indeed, he said he had little time for his homeland and for many of its people.

His father, a heavy drinker, suffered financial problems which depressed the boy. Young Ibsen, a loner, often locked himself away with his puppets, dolls, drawings and books-most often the Bible. The lad enjoyed magic tricks and practised ventriloquism on his three younger brothers. There were occasions when he stood on a barrel from where he made his "speeches" to his siblings. Religion and history were his favourite topics.

Because of family finances, Henrik at age sixteen became an apprentice pharmacist in Grimstad. At age eighteen, this "outsider" begat a son whose servant-girl mother was ten years his senior. Henrik supported his son for thirteen years or more but never saw the child again until he, himself was an old man. After the age of twenty-two Ibsen never saw his parents again, lamenting several times that "my father and my mother never loved me."

Many experts consider Ibsen's plays autobiographical. For example, his first, *Catilina*, contained themes-a destructive mistress, a rebellious hero-that preoccupied him throughout his career. His plays seemingly are dramatizations of his intellectual, social, and emotional life. These were developed with rigorous thought, economy of action, and penetrating dialogue.

Most of his writing was done away from Norway. In 1864, he left for Italy. For the next twenty-seven years he lived abroad-in Italy and elsewhere in Europe with only two brief visits to Norway. 'How one longs for the sun" is an oft-repeated quote in his writings. Often his plays were scorned and hissed by audiences. *Ghosts*, for example, was called "an open drain [and] a loathsome sore, an abominable piece, a repulsive and degrading work," according to a London reviewer and critic. Ibsen earlier commented: "*Ghosts* will probably cause alarm in certain circles, but that cannot be helped. If it did not, it would not have been necessary to write it."

Peer Gynt (1857), an Ibsen classic drama in rhymed couplets, features a buoyant, self-centered, aimless, unprincipled opportunist. Yet there is something loveable about the rascal.

Ibsen's *Doll House* (1879), an unsentimental story of a woman's shattered illusions about loyalty and marriage, is his most famous work. Many other plays (twenty-six in total) flowed from his pen-*An Enemy of the People, The Wild Duck, Hedda Gabler,* the *Masta Builder,* among others. When We Dead Awaken (1899) features an ageing artist who has trouble accepting his failing powers. More autobiography. He returned to Norway in 1891 where he continued his writing until two strokes made him an invalid.

Newspaper reviews of Ibsen's *Ghosts* and *Hedda Gabler* included "...a wave of folly", "...a crazy fanatic", "...a crazy cranky being...not only consistently dirty but deplorably dull", and "...a gloomy sort of ghoul...blinking like a stupid old owl."

On May 16, 1906 Ibsen was in a coma in his bedroom surrounded by friends and relatives. A nurse told the visitors that the playwright seemed a little better. Without opening his eyes, Ibsen uttered his last word: "Tvestimod" (on the contrary).

In spite of his success as a playwright (his work was translated into many languages) Ibsen was careful with his money. He checked and re-checked his royalties and his expenses, including the cost of every cheap cigar. A genuine tightwad.

The man was a heretic, a genius, an original, a rebel, and an individual whose pen continues to amaze, anger and entertain. It was Ibsen who said: "Do not use that foreign word 'ideals'. We have that excellent native word 'lies'."
More Ibsen quotes follow:

-*The strongest man in the world is he who stands most alone.*

-*The man whom God wills to stay in the struggle of life, He first individualizes.*

-*What's a man's first duty? The answer is brief, to be himself.*

-*Friends are a costly luxury, and when one invests one's capital in a mission in life, one cannot afford to have friends.*

-*...the only thing about liberty that I love is the fight for it. I care nothing about the possession of it*

-*I hold that man is in the right who is most closely in league with the future.*

-*The minority is always right...but, damn it, it can surely never be right that the stupid should rule the clever!*

-*One should never have your best trousers on when you go out to fight for freedom and truth.*

-*Really to sin you have to be serious about it.*

ISHAM

After visiting the splendid Gardiner Dam on Lake Diefenbaker, head west on Highway #44 to the *Plato's corner. Dip a little south and then you'll be in Isham.

How many people wear fur coats and hats in Isham? The man after whom the centre was named would be pleased if you would see such apparel.

JAMES ISHAM (1716-1761)

The London-born Hudson Bay Factor, writer and naturalist served the HBC (formed in 1670) from 1732, with four brief visits to England, to his death. His writings remain a strong source for understanding the 18th Century fur trade. Isham's "creative" spelling, grammar and style add flavour. The flora and fauna of Rupert's Land kept his pen busy.

At age twenty-one he took command at York Fort (York Factory) on the Hudson Bay. Earlier he was sent there as a "writer" for the HBC. The competent trader received goods from Indians as far away as Lac Ouinipigon (Lake Winnipeg). During his stay at the Fort-until 1741-he exercised what other naturalists called his "commendable curiosity." He made a collection of "beasts, birds and fishes" as well as the "habits, toys and utensils" of the Indians. The clever man took some of his newly "discovered" (stuffed) to England.

Isham was promoted and sent to lead the company's concerns and business at Churchill from where he was to encourage trade with more northern Indians and Eskimos. Churchill was to be the springboard to the rumoured Coppermine River. However, he found explorers to be a trouble, a bother, a distraction. At Churchill he thrashed and imprisoned some of them to maintain his control. His purpose was trade. His hard work continued in spite of a bronchial condition, a strained groin and lameness caused by gout.

In 1743 he wrote a *Vocabulary of English and Indian, Observations upon Hudson's Bay* and *Small Account of the Northward Indian Language*, among other reports. It seems that those writings received little attention in London.

However his notes on the flora and fauna were valued-and remain a valued pioneer contribution to knowledge.

Isham's "Observations" stressed that the English ought to go inland-as far as present day Cumberland House, Saskatchewan. He also anticipated the plan which, in 1771, took Samuel Hearne to the mouth of the Coppermine River.

In 1751 the trader was sent back to the Fort York area-a move he really didn't appreciate. There he set the pattern that took English traders to the Paskoya (Saskatchewan) River and the prairies. It was he who sent the remarkable Anthony Henday and a band of Crees to the prairies as far west as Siksika (Blackfoot) country. Isham continued to strengthen English trade, countered French trade, and made peace between warring Indians. An acclaimed master to the traders, he was mourned at his death as "the idol of the Indians," perhaps a dubious comment. The shrewd and sound decision-maker, however, caused considerable criticism: Upon his death he left all his property to his half-Indian son. (His English wife had remained in England where she died a year earlier. Their daughter was left to mourn her.) His son, Charles Thomas Price Isham, later became a redoubtable trader and traveller for the HBC.

James Isham: A doer, thinker, organizer, trader, naturalist and writer. He had a useful pen.

* Because the settlement of Plato was named after an American place by that name, Plato, the philosopher, is not included in this book.

ITUNA

(See KIPLING and ITUNA)

KELVINGTON

Head south from the Nipawin-Tisdale area on Highway #35. Stop for gas at Rose Valley and then head east and south a bit to Kelvington. If Lord Kelvin had his way you would be studying your old math and physics texts. Watch for brilliant Scots with strange looking equipment.

BARON KELVIN OF LARGES (1824-1907)

The brilliant Scot physicist and mathematician, William Thomson, was the originator of the absolute (the Kelvin) scale of temperature, and was a founder of thermodynamics. At age twenty-two Thomson was appointed professor of natural philosophy at the university of Glasgow. He held that professorship for fifty-three years. Remarkable! At that university he inaugurated the first British physics laboratory for students.

In 1847 he originated the temperature scale, and four years later he proposed the second law of thermodynamics. By age thirty-one he reached his peak in pure physics. By then he had published ninety-six scientific papers.

For ten years Thomson's research focused on thermoelectric effects, resulting in his discovery of the "Thomson heat effect." He began to study the application of physics to the field of electricity. He wrote many articles on telegraphic signalling by wire which were useful in the laying of the first Atlantic cable.

Professor Thomson developed and patented equipment such as the minor galvonometer, the siphon recorder for telegraphy, the quadrant electrometer and stranded conductors. He became famous and wealthy as a result of his work and inventions. The esteemed researcher was a leading member of the British Committee on Electrical Standards, which was instrumental in the adoption of electrical units used internationally. The kelvin is the unit of absolute temperature. Thus absolure zero is zero kelvin symbolized by OK. Water, which boils at 100C. or 212F. is measured at 373.17K.

In 1866 Thomson was knighted and in 1892 was elevated to the peerage as Baron Kelvin of Largs. Lord Kelvin was often quoted as saying, "If you cannot measure it, then it is not science." The honoured scientist was buried in Westminister Abbey.

KIPLING and ITUNA

Drive east from Regina on the Trans-Canada Highway to Broadview and turn south. Cross the Pipestone Creek and head for Kipling.

But start your visit at Kipling-and be stirred by the writer's ringing verse and pungent prose. You will be in Writers Corner.

The Celtic name for the Solway Firth, north-western England, is Ituna. Kipling's written mention of Ituna led to the naming of that community an hour's drive west of Yorkton.

RUDYARD KIPLING (1865-1936)

The Bombay-born and English-educated Kipling was one of those rare writers equally at home in verse and in prose. At age seventeen, he returned to India where he edited a newspaper. By age twenty-five, he was an acknowledged master of the short story. His stories of the common soldier and sailor opened up a new literary field. Before long he was considered "a poetic press agent" for the British Empire.

The English novelist, poet, and short-story writer is well remembered for his "celebration" of British Imperialism and his stories for adults and children-based in India and Burma. To this day his stories for children-the *Jungle Books, Captains Courageous* (placed on Canada's Grand Banks), and *Just So Stories*-remain popular. In his early twenties he travelled to Japan, China, and America. Writer Henry James was one of the first to feel in Kipling's tales "the irresistible magic of scorching suns, subject empires, uncanny religions, uneasy garrisons". Kipling became famous for his "hard reality". *The Man Who Would Be King, Back Room Ballads*, and *Kim* are examples of his prose writing.

In 1907, he won the Nobel Prize for Literature. The low point in his life was when his teenage soldier-son was killed in World War I. Countless students have memorized *Fuzzy-Wuzzy,* and other Kipling poems. Millions more have sung his 1897 poem, *Recessional*, set to music:

> *The tumult and the shouting dies;*
> *The Captains and the Kings depart:*
> *Still stands Thine ancient sacrifice*
> *An humble and a contrite heart.*
> *Lord God of Hosts be with us yet,*
> *Lest we forget-lest we forget!*

Readers will recall other famous quotations and phrases from Kipling:

> *-Words are, of course, the most powerful drug used by mankind.*
> *-You big black boundin' beggar-for you broke the British square.*
> *-You're a better man than I am, Gunga Din.*
> *-The White Man's burden.*
> *-A woman is only a woman, but a good cigar is a smoke.*
> *-The female of the species is more deadly than the male.*
> *-You may carve it on his tombstone, you may cut it on his card*
> *-That a young man married is a young man marred.*
> *-Oh, East is East and West is West, and never the twain shall meet....*
> *-The sin ye do by two and two ye must pay for one by one.*

A favourite Kipling statement:

> *The style of a man's play, plus the normal range of his vices, divided by the square of his work, and multiplied by the coefficient of his nationality, gives, not only his potential resistance under breaking-strain but indicates, within a few points, how far he may be trusted to pull off a losing game.*

Canadian soldiers today might reflect on Kipling's lines written about Britain's earlier military attempt to secure the Afghanistan region:

> *When you're wounded and left on Afghanistan's plains,*
> *An' the women come to cut up what remains,*
> *Jest roll your rifle an' blow out your brains*
> *And go to your Gawd like a soldier.*

(Kandahar, Saskatchewan, was named after the site of a famous battle won by the British army under Roberts during the Afghanistan War of 1879-1880.)

Kipling had a keen edge to his pen. He wrote that "the American has no language. He has no dialect, slang, provincialism, accent, and so-forth." Kipling saved some of his sharper comments for Medicine Hat, Alberta: "You people in the district seem to have all Hell for a basement."

Kipling's 1897 *Our Lady of the Snows* described Canada's relations with Britain in terms of those of a daughter and a mother. The last verse is as follows:

> *A Nation spoke to a Nation,*
> *A Throne sent word to a Throne"*
> *"Daughter am I in my mother's house,*
> *But mistress in my own.*
> *The gates of mine to open,*
> *As the gates are mine to close,*
> *And I abide in my Mother's House,"*
> *Said our Lady of the Snows.*

Kipling also commented on Western Canada: "The prairie which is the High Veldt, plus Hope, Activity, and Reward."

A newspaper wrongly announced Kipling's death. His written response: "I've just read that I am dead. Don't forget to delete me from your list of subscribers."

At the height of his success, Kipling received a letter from an autograph hunter who enclosed one dollar in the belief that the great man charged a dollar per word. "Please send me a sample," requested the letter writer. Kipling wrote back: "Thanks."

His "imperialist persuasions" grew less popular as time passed. Today many people associate Kipling with the Victorian Age. A typical sharp criticism came from the Welsh poet Dylan thomas: "Mr. Kipling...stands for everything in this cankered world which I would wish were otherwise."

One wonders how many Saskatchewan students, among others, struggled through "*Kim*" and memorized the famous poem "*If*".

Kipling: A literary giant. It was he who wrote:

I had six honest serving men,
They taught me all I know;
Their names were Where and What and When
And Why and How and Who.

LAMPMAN

Enjoy the outdoors as you travel to another centre honouring a Canadian poet who would enjoy those outdoors as much as anyone else. Lampman is your goal in southeastern Saskatchewan, about thirty miles north east of Estevan. Another substantial addition to Writers Corner.

ARCHIBALD LAMPMAN (1861-1899)

Many experts consider Lampman the finest 19th Century Canadian poet. The civil servant (he unhappily worked in the Post office Department in Ottawa) was known as on of the "Confederation"poets. Born in Canada's West's Morpeth, he later obtained a B.A. at Toronto's Trinity College. He had been introduced to poetry by his father, a classical scholar. Young Lampman read the Greek tragic poets in Greek. He admired the English poets Wordsworth, Keats, Arnold and Milton.

The moody, shy and somewhat reclusive Lampman had a small circle of friends-intellectuals and writers-in Ottawa. On occasion, he read papers and poetry to various scientific and literary groups. Perhaps his sonnets were and are best appreciated. The public learned that the strikingly handsome Lampman was at the height of his power when contemplating and observing nature, where, like Wordsworth, he found spiritual strength.

The young poet's poor health and the death of his young son seem to have led to his spiritual malaise. During one of his many camping trips to the woodlands, he over-strained his heart.

Four years before his death, he was elected "Fellow of the Royal Society of Canada". He loved his homeland but he wrote this lament: "How utterly destitute of all light and charm are the intellectual conditions of our people and the institutions of our public life. How barren! How barbarous!"

However, Lampman also wrote poetry with a positive note. Part of *The Largest Life* is as follows:

There is a beauty at the goal of life,
A beauty growing since the world began,
Through every age and race, through lapse and strife,
Till the great human soul completes her span

Admirers of Lampman's poetry can also enjoy his *Heat, Solitude, Midnight, In November, Winter Evening, The City of the End of Things* (a sombre allegory of human life), *The Truth, Among the Millet, The Violinist,* among many others. Life's unfairness is expressed clearly in Lampman's *To a Millionaire.*

Repelled by the mechanization of urban life, Lampman's poetry sensitively records the feelings evoked by the incidents and scenes he found in his beloved outdoors.

With a very sharp pen, Lampman wrote *The Modern Politician*:

> *What manner of soul is his to whom high truth*
> *Is but the plaything of a feverish hour,*
> *A dangling ladder to the ghost of power!*
> *Gone are the grandeurs of the world's iron youth,*
> *When kings were mighty, being made by swords.*
>
> *Now comes the transit age, the age of brass,*
> *Blinding the multitude with specious words.*
> *To them faith, kinship, truth and verity*
> *Men's sacred rights are very holiest thing,*
>
> *Are but the counters at a desperate play,*
> *Flippant and reckless what the end may be,*
> *So that they glitter, each his little day,*
> *The little mimic of a vanquished king.*

(Do you know any politician "to whom high truth is but a plaything"?)

With poetry, Lampman honoured the heroism of Adam Dollard des Ormeaux (Dollard, west of Shauvanon, is named after him) who, with seventeen soldiers saved Ville Marie (later called Montreal) from the Iroquois in 1660. After ten days of fighting, near today's Cornwall, all the men were killed or captured. Lampman's *At the Long Sault : May 1660* should be considered a Canadian classic:

Silent, white-faced, again and again
Charged and hemmed round by furious hands,
Each for a moment faces them all and stands
In his little desperate ring; like a tired bull moose
Whom scores of sleepless wolves, a ravening pack,
Have chased all night, all day
Through snow-laden woods, like famine let loose;
As he turns at last in his track
Against a wall of rock and strands at bay;
Round him with terrible sinews and teeth of steel
They charge and recharge; but with many a furious
plunge and wheel,
Hither and thither over the trampled snow,
He tosses them bleeding and torn;
Till, driven, and ever to and fro
Harried. Wounded and weary grown,
His mighty strength gives way
And all together they fasten upon him and drag him
down.

Further Lampman thoughts:

--I love the face of every man whose thought is swift
and sweet.
-The frost that stings like fire upon my cheek....
...and wintry grief is a forgotten guest.
-Children of Silence and Eternity,
-They know no season but the end of time.
-Of bipeds, all the way down
To the pimp and the politician.
I saw the haggard dreadfulness
Of old age and death.
-When the strength of man is shattered,
And the powers of earth are scattered,
From beneath the ghostly ruin
Peace shall rise.

LIPTON

Of course, you will stop for tea at Lipton, a one hour drive north-east of Regina. Take Highway #10 for a very pleasant drive to Fort Qu'Appelle. Your thirst will be quenched if you head for Lipton, a few minutes away. What brand of tea will you request?

THOMAS JOHNSON LIPTON (1850-1931)

Lipton knew full well that the America's Cup had the greatest public fame of all yachting competitions. He didn't give up easily. Here are his results:

Year	Winning Yacht	Owner	Challenger	Owner
1899	Columbia	C. Iselin &	Shamrock	Sir T. Lipton syndicate
1901	Columbia	J.P. Morgan	Shamrock 11	Sir T. Lipton
1903	Reliance	C. Iselin &	Shamrock 111	Sir T. Lipton syndicate
1920	Resolute	C. Vanderbilt	Shamrock 1V	Sir T. Lipton & syndicate
1930	Enterprise	H. Vanderbilt	Shamrock V	Sir T. Lipton & syndicate

Obviously only the very rich could enter such competitions.

T.J. Lipton had become a very rich man, indeed. Born to Irish parents in Glasgow, Lipton's first job was as an errand-boy to a local stationer. At age fifteen, he moved to USA where he clerked in a grocery store, drove a streetcar in New Orleans, became a salesman for a portrait firm, and worked on a South Carolina plantation.

The enterprising young man returned to Glasgow where he opened a small provision shop. He was successful so he expanded. Eventually he had shops all over Scotland and in many parts of USA.

His wealth allowed him to purchase plantations in Ceylon which produced excellent cocoa, coffee and tea. In

England he established fruit farms, jam factories, bacon-curing establishments and bakeries. He also had a very successful packinghouse for hogs in Chicago. Lipton had become a very wealthy individual.

His reputation and financial power led to his 1898 knighthood from Queen Victoria. Four years later he was made a baronet.

Lipton's determination was never in question. Five times he tried to win the America's Cup. He lost five times. True to his Irish roots he named his competing yachts "Shamrock."

He used his pen to good advantage. Lipton helped to design those yachts. Countless hours were spent over paper and pen. His correspondence with other leading industrialists makes him a man of the pen.

The successful entrepreneur left part of his fortune to the poor mothers and children of Glasgow.

LUXTON and MACKLIN

The *Manitoba Free Press* is "connected" to two more Saskatchewan settlements Luxton is a long newspaper toss away from Lampman, a few minutes drive north-east of Estevan, deep in Writers Corner. Later you can take a long drive through Regina, north on the divided Highway #11, west on #15 to Kindersley and then a short haul north-west to Macklin near the Alberta border. Here is splendid goose hunting country.

In both Luxton and Macklin you can expect to be interviewed. Will bad language be involved?

WILLIAM FISHER LUXTON (1844-1907)

Eleven-year-old William left England for Canada. He was sad about leaving his pals and other relatives but was very excited about moving to a "new country." After his schooling was finished, he tried teaching for a short time. At age twenty-two he began his newspaper career. He established and edited several Ontario newspapers.

Volume 1 Number 1 of the *Manitoba Free Press* was launched November 30, 1872 by two young men: William Luxton, who had the experience, and John A. Kenny, who had the muscle and the money. Luxton used the printing press he had purchased in New York. The type and press arrived by Red River steamboat. At first the cylinder press was run by the muscles of young Kenny, a large and powerful individual.

The eight-page first edition's main story was the re-election of USA President Ulysses S. Grant. It also carried classified ads, local news, a poem, a story, telegraphic dispatches and editorials. The nine hundred subscribers paid twenty-five cents per week. The young Luxton and Kenny had many challenges including an unsure source and delivery of newsprint, failure of telegraphic service and tough working conditions.

However, the newspaper's growing subscription rates and increased advertising revenue allowed the owners to move several times to better working conditions and equipment. The paper's motto "Freedom of Trade, Liberty of Religion and Equality of Civil Rights" was well received. Luxton's outspoken editorials helped to shape public opinion: Luxton was Winnipeg's booster.

By 1892, control of the paper shifted to Clifford Sifton. Later, for over forty years, John Dafoe served as president, writer and editor-in-chief. (see elsewhere in this book for Dafoe information.) Another worthy employee was Harry Macklin, a business manager well-known for his sulphuric vocabulary and quick temper. Macklin followed the progress of the growth of the GTP railway and regularly wrote his reports for the *Manitoba Free Press*, later (1931) called the

Winnipeg Free Press. The town of Macklin is named in his honour.

Today the streets of Macklin, Saskatchewan carry the names of earlier newspapers: *Herald, Tribune, Empire, Times, Post, Telegraph* and *Leader.*

Consider the power of the pen and press.

MACOUN

A short hop north-west on Highway #39 from Estevan will bring you to Macoun. Few centres are named for people who had more impact on and love for the area called Saskatchewan.

Macoun: Proud member of Writers Corner.

JOHN MACOUN (1831-1920)

The 1872 shoot near Quill Lake was successful, and the men cleaned, cooked and ate several whooping cranes. Sanford Fleming's men were searching out a route for the proposed Canadian Pacific Railway. At least one member of the expedition, the explorer-teacher-author-civil servant-botanist-naturalist John Macoun (pronounced Macown) lived to regret such a meal. It was the first of five government surveys between 1872 and 1881 in which Macoun worked with Fleming.

The Irish-born Macoun, fatherless at age six, developed a passion for Ireland's outdoors. He grew to become a rather pompous young man who considered himself morally superior because of his "obvious virtues." He believed he was seldom wrong. The Ulsterman strongly supported the British crown and the Orange Order.

In 1850 the Macoun family moved to Canada where the young man tried teaching and later served as a volunteer during the 1866 Fenian troubles. He developed a serious interest in the local flora.

Macoun (MA Syracuse University) was to amass a collection of Canadian fauna and flora which became the foundation for the National Museum of Natural Science. During his trips west, he displayed a special love for the beautiful Saskatchewan Lily (*Lilium philadephicum*) which grew wild in patches of an acre or more. Near Last Mountain Lake, which he called "the Flower Garden of the North West" he also found countless large and delicious mushrooms. Because he saw so many gulls there, he named another area Gull Lake (another writer-connected name place).

The tireless Macoun, "the professor" as he was popularly called, provided agricultural justification for the CPR's southern route. Later the outspoken plant geographer was named Dominion botanist, and he established the Dominion Herbarium of over 100,000 species. He discovered over one thousand of them. He was delighted when, in 1882, he was named a charter member of the Royal Society of Canada.

The distinguished Canadian with his heavy white eyebrows, moustache and beard was widely recognized in scientific circles. He was proud when his son, John William (1869-1933) became the first Dominion Horticulturist.

The elder Macoun, optimist and enthusiast, corrected some of the earlier impressions of the west and especially of the area now called Saskatchewan. He scorned Darwinism and he believed that a naturalist should be a "jack of all fields" rather than a "specialist". The naturalist's job, he maintained, was to assemble an accurate and complete inventory of "God's wondrous bounty."

Not all experts agreed with Macoun, however. For example, in 1883 his superior and Deputy Minister of the Interior, Lindsay Russell, called Macoun "a good specialist and honest fool outside of that."

In spite of such comment, Macoun clearly added tremendous knowledge to Canadiana. Ernest Thompson Seton, world renowned naturalist, said Macoun was "the pioneer naturalist of Canada." He pushed back the frontiers of our natural history.

MAIR

Why did those settlers name their district after a man who lived in the times of Christopher Columbus (1451?-1506), Ignatius Loyola (1491-1556) and Martin Luther (1483-1546)? Did some individual become impressed with the Latin writings of philosopher-theologian John Mair?

The settlement is another worthy member of Writers Corner. Travel east on Highway #1 and turn south at Moosomin on Highway #8 for thirty minutes or so to the Mair district. Be in a very serious mood.

JOHN MAIR (1470-1550)

The Scottish writer and thinker was born at Gleghornie, educated at Haddington School, studied briefly at Cambridge and then at the University of Paris where he received a Master of Arts in 1496. Mair (or Major) was "promoted" to the doctorate in 1503.

In 1518 Mair was appointed principal regent at the University of Glasgow. Seven years later he moved to St. Andrews University where, except for a brief time in Paris, he spent the rest of his academic career. All his writings were in Latin. Among other items, he wrote an introduction to Aristotle's logic, commentaries on *Matthew,* another commentary on the Four Gospels, and the famous *Historia Majoris Britanniae* (1521) in which, among other ideas, he encouraged royal intermarriages with a view to a peaceful union between Scotland and England. (The Act of Union wasn't passed until 1707.)

In political philosophy, Mair maintained the Scottish position that civil authority is derived from the popular will. Although he supported Gallicanism's plea for ecclesiastical reform he remained a scholastic conservative. "Theological peace" was important to Mair.

The scholar believed that a historian's chief responsibility is to write truthfully. Perhaps it was a bit self-serving of him to suggest that that responsibility could best be met by a theologian. His voluminous writings are usually grouped under history, scripture commentary, logic and philosophy.

Two of Mair's most famous students were George Buchanan (1506-1582) and John Knox (1505?-1572).

MASEFIELD

Enjoy your one-and-one-half hour drive south of Swift Current on Highway #4. When you get ten minutes north of the US border ask for the settlement known as Masefield, likely named after one the most popular and beloved modern poets.

A prairie district named for a man of the sea? A resounding yes! So many fine sailors have come from the prairies.

JOHN MASEFIELD (1898-1967)

Masefield, born in Ledbury, central England, lost his father early so the youngster ran away from home to become a sailor-vagabond who visited the four corners of the earth. The sea always had glamour for Masefield. The youth worked in America for a few years as a bartender, farm hand and factory labour, (Years later, in 1941 he wrote *In the Mill*, an autobiography which tells of his work in a carpet factory.)

John Masefield got his education from his heavy reading-mostly in English literature. The worker-bookworm began to write his own poetry.

Five years after his return to England, Masefield published *Salt-Water Ballads* (1902), a collection of lively lyrics of the sea and sailors. Critics later praised his work for its Chaucerian vigour, its plain speech and rhythmical heartiness! *The Everlasting Mercy* (1911), among his other narrative poems, shocked the literary establishment with its phrases of a colloquial coarseness not found elsewhere in early 20th Century English verse. The popularity of Masefield's "rude" and sometimes shocking story poems was very high indeed. Perhaps his best work is to be found in his *Collective Poems* (1932). He also wrote more than a dozen plays.

Some observers believed Masefield's *Reynard the Fox* (1919), which vigorously expresses the spirit of rural England, led to his 1930 appointment as Poet Laureate.

His other works includes novels of adventure, stories for children and a second autobiography, *So Long to Learn* (1932).

Masefield's *Sea Fever* remains popular today:

> I must go down to the seas again, to the lonely sea
> And the sky,
> And all I ask is a tall ship and a star to steer her by,
> And the wheel's kick and the wind's song and the
> White sail's shaking,
> And the gray mist on the sea's face and a gray dawn
> Breaking....

A Wanderer's Song expresses his earlier-mentioned romance with the sea:

> A wind's in the heart of me, a fire's in my heels,
> I am tired of brick and stone and the rumbling wagon-
> wheels;
> I hunger for the sea's edge, the limits of the land,
> Where the wild old Atlantic is shouting on the sand.

In a more sombre and reflective mood, Masefield wrote *On Growing Old*.

Be with me, beauty, for the fire is dying,
My dog and I are old, too old for roving.
Man, whose young passion sets the spendthrift flying,
Is soon too lame to march, too cold for loving...

I cannot sail your seas, I cannot wander
Your cornland, nor your hill-land, nor your
    Valleys
Ever again, nor share the battle of yonder
Where the young knight the broken squadron rallies...

John Masefield wrote about hunters, labourers, sailors and murderers. His topics and his talents seem rooted in the fact he knew what constitutes a good day's work among unpretentious workers. Some of his quotes follow:

-And fifteen arms went round her waist.
(And then men ask, "Are Barmaids chaste?")
-Coming in solemn beauty like slow old tunes of Spain.
Death opens unknown doors. It is most grand to die.
-It is good to be out on the road, and going one knows
not where.
-But the loveliest things of beauty God ever showed to
me,
Are her voice, and her hair, and eyes, and the dear red
curve of her lips.
Over the grasses of the ancient way
Rutted this morning by the passing guns.
-It's a warm wind, the west wind, full of bird's cries;
I never hear the west wind but tears are in my eyes.

MAXWELTON

A lovely poem. An evocative ballad. A tender love song. You'll be singing *Maxwelton Braes* or *Annie Laurie* as it is more often called.

Get your loved one ready. Drive south from Moose Jaw on Highway #624 until you re*ach* the community just north of Willow Bunch Lake. The Maxwelton post office is no more. However, you know the melody. Hum or sing softly and tenderly. Your loved one will be impressed.

Will you allow Maxwelton to be part of Writers Corner? A tough call.

MAXWELTON

Annie was a beauty. And she knew it. She was the youngest of seven children born to Sir Robert Laurie and his wife, Jean. The family lived happily at Maxwelton on the banks of the Cairn River, Dumfriesshire, Scotland.

The beautiful Annie Laurie won the heart of William Douglas, an ex-soldier (Captain) of the Royal Scots-a young man who had earned his reputation for bravery. Annie, born in 1682, had grown into a bit of a flirt. William and Annie met at a ball in Edinburgh where an instant attraction became evident. Later they secretly met often in the woods and braes around Maxwelton. William fell for the beautiful girl.

Alas, the young man was called back for army duty, and he left for the continent. The night before he left, he penned these words:

> Maxwelton braes are bonnie,
> Where early fa's the dew;
> An' it's here that Annie Laurie
> Gi'ed me her promise true;
> Gi'ed me her promise true,
> Which ne'er forgot shall be;
> And for Annie Laurie
> I'll lay me doun and die.

The love-struck young man went on to describe sweet Annie:

> Her brow is like the snaw-drift,
> Her throat is like the swan,

Her face it is the fairest
That e'er the sun shone on;
That e'er the sun shone on—
An' dark blue is her e'e;
An' for bonnie Annie Laurie
I'd lay me doun and dee.

And did Annie cry herself to sleep after William departed? Was she inconsolable for his loss? No! No! Annie Laurie had several love affairs while soldier-boy was away. There is no record of the two sending letters to each other. Annie gave up adoration for financial security: she married the wealthy Alexander Ferguson of Craigdarroch. The graceful, slender, brown-haired, blue-eyed Annie was a beautiful bride. As far as anyone knows, she and Alexander were happy and well-suited. In a letter she later referred to her earlier poet-lover: "I hope that he is content." Rather dismissive.

William Douglas returned home. There is no proof that he and Annie ever met again. Later he married Elizabeth Clerc of Glenburg by whom he had four sons and two daughters.

Annie meanwhile raised her family, tended her formal georgian gardens, became something of a matchmaker (she knew how to select husbands?) and wrote her many letters. She outlived her husband by many years before going to her own grave in 1761 at age seventy-nine.

Today one can see Annie's grave at Craigdarroch and her painted portraits at Maxwelton.

Years later one Lady John Scott claimed that she wrote the tune for *Annie Laurie,* changed the second verse and added a third, as follows:

Like dew on gowan lying
Is the fa' o' her fairy feet;
Like simmer breezes sighing,
Her voice is low an' sweet;
Her voice is low an' sweet—
An' she's a' the world to me;

An' for Annie Laurie
I'd lay me doun and dee.

Published anonymously, as was the custom with most female authors of the day, the lilting song was made public in 1838. (It is likely that Lady Scott also wrote *The Bonnie Banks of Loch Lomond*.) She obviously had no idea that her song would become so popular.

However, *Annie Laurie* was written by a person deeply in love. Or was it written by a fellow with mere puppy love, as some cynics suggest?

Those cynics should not be quickly dismissed. No one knows how much the above account is true-or merely traditional. Perhaps it doesn't matter: We have those lovely notes and words.

McGEE
(see D'Arcy and McGee)

MINNEHAHA AND NOKOMIS

These two settlements were named in honour of characters found in Longfellow's poem, *Hiawatha.*

Take the pleasant drive from North Battleford north west on Highways #4 and #26. There you will get directions to the area once served by a post office called Minnehaha. Watch for a talented long fellow.

Or perhaps you would rather travel south east from Saskatoon on Highway #16 to Lanigan and then south on #20 to Nokomis. Consult a certain old and wise grandmother.

In which area, Minnehaha or Nokomis will you find "Laughing Waters"?

HENRY WADSWORTH LONGFELLOW (1807-1882)

Longfellow, the most popular American poet of the 19th Century, graduated from Maine's Bodoin College in

1825. He then travelled extensively in Europe and returned in 1829 to his home college as a librarian and professor. His later professorship in Harvard allowed him research time in Heidelberg, Germany, where he was deeply influenced by German romanticism.

After his return to Harvard he published widely including *Evangeline* (1847), a highly popular idyll of the former French colony of Acadia (Nova Scotia and neighbouring areas). He left university work in 1854 and a year later he published *Hiawatha* (Laughing Waters), a long narrative poem noted for its use of trochaic meter. He wrongly "placed" Hiawatha too far west. (In fact the chief ca. 1450 of the Onondaga tribe lived well to the east.) However, that work, among many other of his poems, has remained popular to today.

Longfellow's *Hiawatha* is an Ojibwa Indian raised by Nokomis, his wise old grandmother. The mature Hiawatha wants to avenge the wrong done by the West Wind, his father, who had hurt the youth's mother. Eventually the son and father have reconciliation.

Hiawatha becomes his people's leader and he marries Minnehaha of the former enemy Dakota tribe. Under Hiawatha's leadership an era of learning and peace takes place.

Later, however, famine and disease strike the people. Many people including Hiawatha die as a result. Before his death he told his people to heed those who will come with a new religion. Then the great chief, according to the Longfellow poem, left for the Isles of the Blessed.

Perhaps the best known lines from the poem, *Hiawatha* are as follows:

> *By the shores of Gitche Gumee,*
> *By the shining Big-Sea Water,*
> *Stood the wigwam of Nokomis,*
> *Daughter of the Moon, Nokomis.*

The sing-song meter of the poem has led to many parodies. Some cruel. Many in bad taste. Yes, Longfellow had his opponents. Consider what American critic Van Wyck Brooks said: "Longfellow is to poetry what the barrel-organ is to music."

However, Longfellow's *Hiawatha*, Minnehaha and Nokomis have the last word. They have become part of our language and story telling. Some of his words follow here:

-Art signifies no more than this. Art is power.

-Art is the revelation of man; and not merely that, but likewise the revelation of nature, speaking through man.

-A boy's will is the wind's will.

-Were half the power that fills the world with terror,
Were half the wealth bestowed on camps and courts,
Given to redeem the human mind from error,
There were no need for arsenals or forts.

-A life that is worth writing at all, is worth writing minutely and truthfully.

-It has done me good to be somewhat parched by the heat and drenched by the rain of life.

-This world loves a spice of wickedness.

-Whenever nature leaves a hole in a person's mind, she generally plasters it over with a thick coat of self-deceit.

-Lives of great men all remind us
We can make our lives sublime,
And, departing, leave bhind us
Footprints in the sands of time.

MOZART

On your next trip between Saskatoon and Yorkton, pull your vehicle off Highway #16 at the Mozart corner. Note the names of the streets: Liszt, Chopin, Wagner.

Of course, you know what music to bring to your pleasant journey. Lean back in your car seat, adjust the volume and listen to the sounds created by sheer genius. Enjoy.

WOLFGANG AMADEUS MOZART (1756-1791)

"Before God, and as an honest man, I tell you that your son is the greatest composer known to me." Those words were spoken by the famous composer Joseph Haydn to the father of Wolfgang. (Hollywood has called him Amadeus.)

The Austrian-born genius created music perhaps more widely respected and loved than any other composer. Mozart's music has a unique mixture of universality and individuality. He wrote in every genre known to him.

At age two, as the story goes, young Mozart heard a pig squeal. "G sharp!" he shouted. Someone went to the piano and G sharp was correct. He was born with perfect pitch. At age three the boy could pick out chords on the piano, and by age five he was improvising short minuets on the keyboard. When he was six his ambitious father (also a composer and writer of a textbook on violin playing) took the boy and his precocious sister, Nannerl, to Munich to perform. The youngsters were a great success. There is the famous story about the little Mozart falling down on a slippery floor. Seven year old Marie Antoinette picked him up. The boy kissed the future queen and told her: "You are good. I will marry you."

Encouraged by success, the father took the two children on tour to major German cities, Paris and London. They arrived home in Salzburg after three and one half years on tour. Mozart learned from other masters during that tour.

Under the tutelage of his father, Leopold (court musician to the archbishop of Salzburg), the boy became a child prodigy at the violin, organ and harpsichord. Composer Johann Adolph Hasse commented: "This boy [the fifteen year old Mozart] will cause us all to be forgotten." By age seventeen, the youth has mastered all the genres most useful to a composer. His travels and his study in many European centres added to his knowledge and insight.

After a long wait he became the imperial chamber musician and court composer in 1787. Earlier he was fired by the archbishop after a quarrel. Wolfgang experienced considerable poverty in his short life: His "freelance years" provided him with more financial difficulties.

During one visit to Mannheim (which had the most famous orchestras of Europe) he fell in love with the German girl, Aloysia Weber. There he learned much about orchestration-especially the use of clarinets-but he lost the girl. Mozart's father intervened and moved the son and his mother to Paris.

Later, in 1782, Mozart married Constanze Weber, sister of Aloysia. Their first child died soon after birth. Constanze later gave birth to Carl (1784) and Franz (1791). The family continued to have financial problems. Both Mozart and his wife were poor financial managers.

In spite of his erratic behavior and difficulties, Mozart continued to produce music for the world-music of many kinds. He said: "I write as a sow piddles." However, most experts suggest that opera was his greatest interest. Among others, the genius wrote *Idomeneo* (1781), *The Marriage of Figaro* (1786), *Don Giovanni* (1787) and *The Magic Flute* (1791). He wrote many symphonies. Three of his best were written in the space of three months in 1788.

It has been suggested that Mozart's appreciation of the subtler shades of character and mood makes him the theatre's most human composer. The breadth of his artistic imagination leaves one astounded. A more careful observation was made by writer and critic William Hazlitt; "What makes the difference between the opera of Mozart's and the singing of a thrush in a wooden cage at the corner of the street? The one is nature, and the other is art; the one is paid for, and the other is not."

The thirty-five year old Wolfgang Amadeus Mozart was buried in a pauper's grave in Vienna. The world owes him a debt of gratitude. Yet observer Musikelische

Monatschrift could write: "Nobody will fail to see in Mozart a man of talent and an experienced, abundant and agreeable composer. But I have as yet encountered no thorough connoisseur of art who took him for a concert...artist...least of all with tasteful criticism regard him in the matter of poetry, as a true and sensitive composer." A minority report!

A 1763 German newspaper notice (translation) played heavily upon the brilliance of the young, seven-year-old performer:

> *POSITIVELY THE LAST CONCERT! ...THE BOY, NOT YET SEVEN, WILL PERFORM ON THE HARPSICHORD, PLAY A CONCERTO FOR VIOLIN, AND ACCOMPANY SYMPHONIES ON THE CLAVIER, THE KEYBOARD BEING COVERED WITH A CLOTH, AS EASILY AS IF HE COULD SEE ALL THE KEYS. HE WILL NAME ALL NOTES SOUNDED AT A DISTANCE, SINGLY OR IN CHORDS, AND IMPROVISE ON HARPSICHORD AND ORGAN AS LONG AS DESIRED.*

The brilliant, modern wit and pianist Victor Borge commented in jest: "Since he was a little on the lazy side, Mozart didn't start writing opera until he was twelve." Borge added: "Ah Mozart! He was happily married but his wife wasn't."

Other notes on Mozart:

> *-Mozart was born with absolute pitch, infallible sense of rhythm, and natural comprehension in harmony.*
> *-The Emperor of Austria suggested that a Mozart work has "far too many notes." Mozart replied: "Sire, there are just as many notes as there should be."*
> *-People who were to attend Mozart's burial were turned back by a vicious storm. The hearse went on alone. Into an open pit, among the decaying remains of vagrants, prostitutes, criminals and suicides was flung the body of the musical genius.*
> *-At Sotheby's in London on May 22nd, 1997 and autographed manuscript of nine symphonies by Mozart*

were sold for $3,854,500 (U.S.)-a record for such an item.

-If you were to play all of Mozart's music "correctly" it would take you two hundred and two hours.

-A Mozart quote: "Nevertheless, the passions, whether violent or not, should never be so expressed as to reach the point of causing disgust; and music, even in situations of the greatest horror, should never be painful to the ear but should flatter and charm it, an thereby always remain music."

The last words of the musical genius Frederic Chopin were "play Mozart in memory of me." Beethoven studied Mozart diligently. Haydn imitated Mozart. The world remains spellbound.

PARKMAN

Writers Corner also features Parkman, next door to Cannington Manor Provincial Historical Park, just east of Moose Mountain Provincial Park. Anyone who has written as much about Canadian and American history deserves a place named in his/her honour. Think about buffalo hunts, Indian cultures, outdoor living, conflict and scholarship when you next visit Parkman.

FRANCIS PARKMAN (1823-1893)

At age twenty-six, Parkman published the famous book, *The Oregon Trail*. Earlier his scholarly Boston family had instilled in him the love of learning. The Harvard graduate made a trip west where he studied the cultures of various Indian tribes. For some time he lived in a Sioux community. He became a skilled rifleman and canoeist, and learned much about winter survival in the wilderness. Many buffalo fell to the hunter. When he returned to the East his health gave out so he dictated his book to his cousin.

Parkman had an intense interest in the long struggle of the English and French for supremacy in North America. In spite of ill health and near blindness, he spent nearly half a century investigating that earlier struggle.

The man was a wonderful story-teller. However, his books were based on careful research of the facts. Most readers would agree that his interpretations, however, had a Protestant Anglo-Saxon bias. He saw the "competition" as that between liberty and authoritarianism. Among the seven volumes he produced between 1865 and 1892 were the well-known *Pioneers of France in the New World* and *Montcalm and Wolfe* in which he claimed: "In truth the funeral of Montcalm was the funeral of New France."

The historian-hunter-soldier and future President, Theodore (Teddy) Roosevelt was inspired by Parkman's histories.

Well respected are Parkman's studies of the early Northwest United States and Canada, notably *Pioneers of the New World, The Discovery of the Great West, The Old Regime in Canada. A Half-Century of Conflict.* In his *France and England* he wrote: "Spanish civilization crushed the Indian; English civilization scorned and neglected him; French civilization embraced and cherished him." Debatable for sure. He also noted that "a happier calamity never befell as people than the conquest of Canada by the British arms." More debate!

More Parkman quotes:

-Faithfulness to the truth of history involves far more than a research into special facts...the narrator must...himself be, as it were, a sharer or a spectator of the action he describes.

-He (Lasalle) contained his own complex and painful nature the chief springs of his triumphs, his failures, and his death.

PICKTHALL

Pickthall just misses being in Saskatchewan's Writers Corner. Too bad! From Moose Jaw travel south-west on Highway #2 through Assiniboia and then south to Scout Lake. A stone's throw to the north-west you will find the settlement once known as Pickthall.

Watch for well-dressed, demure ladies with slightly crooked, but charming smiles.

MARJORIE L.C. PICKTHALL (1883-1922)

Beautiful large eyes, wide-apart, strong chin set on an oval face with a crooked smile all belong to the photograph of Marjorie L.C. Pickthall, the creator of some of Canada's most poignantly beautiful poetry. Yea, her poetry and her eyes make one think of beauty.

Pickthall moved with the family from London to Toronto in 1889 where she attended the Bishop Strachan School for Girls. Later she worked in the library of Victoria College in the University of Toronto where she assisted in a compilation of Canadian poetry. Her first stories and poems were published when she was fifteen years old. (Over her career, she wrote several hundred short stories and five novels.) Her mother's death in 1910 devastated the young writer who returned to England from 1912 to 1920 where her writing continued with success.

The poetess-writer lived near Salisbury and in London. *The Drift of Pinions* (1913) and *The Map of Poor*

Souls (1916) brought her further recognition. The earlier collection included *Dream River*:

> *O, every morn the winds are stilled,*
> *The sunlight falls in amber bars.*
> *O every night the pools are filled*
> *With silver brede of shaken stars.*
> *O, every morn the sparrow flings*
> *His elfin trills athwart the hush,*
> *And here unseen at eve there sings*
> *One crystal-throated hermit-thrush.*

In the same collection, Pickthall in *The Shepherd Boy* captures the sense of loneliness one can experience:

> *...And whether I lay me near or far*
> *No lip shall kiss me,*
> *No eye shall miss me,*
> *Save the eye of a cold white star.*

During WW I, Pickthall also worked in a meteorological office library, trained as an ambulance driver, and did some farming. Shortly after the war she seemed to be wrestling with her identity. In a letter she wrote:

> *To me the trying part is being a woman at all. I've come to the ultimate conclusion that I'm a misfit of the worst kind, in spite of a superficial femininity—emotion with a foreknowledge of impermanence, a daring mind with only the tongue as an outlet, a greed for experience plus a slavery to convention—what the deuce are you to make of that?—as a woman? As a man, you could go ahead and stir things up fine.*

(Today's feminists are in a position to interpret Pickthall's intent?)

Pickthall was pleased to return to Canada in 1920. For a while she lived with her father in Toronto before settling in a cottage on Vancouver Island. In her poem *When Winter Comes* she describes the area:

Rain at Muchalat, rain at Sooke,
And rain, they say, from Yale to Sheena,
And the skid roads blind, and never a look
Of the Coast Range blue over Malaspina,
And west winds keener
Than jack-knife blades,
And rocks grown greener
With the long drip-drip from the cedar shades....

Early in 1922, the gifted woman died unexpectedly from an embolus. Her father subsequently helped to see that more of her work was published. Perhaps *The Woodcutter's Wife and Later Poems* contains the best of her writings-a story of deep love, betrayal and death is included.

Pickthall's work was later praised by the reviewer-critic Isabel Ecclastone Mackay:

-Besides this quiet yet deep belief in the sanctity of her work, Miss Pickthall possessed an originality of mind and a genius for rare and perfect phrasing....

-...Miss Pickthall very early grasped the happy fact that in the poet's winged imaginings lies the sure way of escape....

-To her, a sense of humour was always the saving grace [but]...tears were for secret places but laughter shared with a friend was a bond which made a closer bond more possible.

It is sad that the work of Marjorie Pickthall is not better known in Canada. Some of her lovely quotes are:

-Oh keep the world for ever at the dawn....
-Praise is pleasant, but I never seem able to apply it to myself.
-They brought Him incense, myrrh and gold,
Our little Lord who lived of old.
-Lovely the day, when light is robed in Splendour,

Walking the ways of God and
Strong with wine:
But the pale eve is wonderful and
Tender,
And night is more divine.
-Too dear for death to dim, or life cast down.
...Our Canada,
From snow to sea,
One hope, one home, one shining destiny!

PITMAN

It seems so right that a master and creator of shorthand has a settlement named in his honour in Writers Corner.

You will find Pitman a short jot south-east of Moose Jaw on Highway #39. Take your pencil and paper: Expect to be "dictated to" by the locals.

ISAAC PITMAN (1813-1897)

Isaac wasn't a strong boy, and he was subject to fainting fits perhaps caused by claustrophobia. At age eleven, he left school and became a clerk in a counting house. There were few other jobs available for him in Trowbridge, Wiltshire, England, his birthplace. His office hours were six to six, a twelve-hour day.

It is reported that young Isaac and his brother Jacob rose at four each morning to study on their own. Another two hours were spent that way each evening after work, according to the report. It was also stated that during his morning walks, Isaac memorized the first fourteen chapters of Proverbs.

In 1837 the young man opened a private school at Wotton-under-Edge where he taught shorthand and other subjects. A friend suggested that he should "invent" his own system of shorthand. (Shorthand: any brief, rabid system of writing that may be used in transcribing the spoken word. Such systems, their characters based on letters of the alphabet, were used even in ancient times.) Perhaps Pitman's speech difficulties helped him to agree with the suggestion.

Pitman's shorthand system is based on phonetic rather than orthographic principles. His publication *Stenographic Soundhand* (1837) brought him fame and considerable money. However, it seems certain that he had no idea that he had invented something that was to revolutionize the world of writing. He once said, "I have no intention of becoming a shorthand author."

This man who underestimated his own impact was knighted in 1894 by Queen Victoria. On a house on Orchard Street, Wotton-on Edge a plaque was placed to identify Isaac Pitman as a local teacher and as the founder of a shorthand system learned by millions.

Isaac's brother, Ben (1822-1910), successfully introduced the shorthand system to America.

PRENDERGAST

After you catch your limit at Meadow Lake, head a bit east to Prendergast. You will be wise to obey the law when you are in the settlement named in honour of a Supreme Court judge.

JAMES EMILE PIERRE PRENDERGAST (1859-1945)

He was a judge who consistently displayed humility, dignity and kindliness on the bench. He earned his reputation as a chivalrous opponent and skilful debater when he was a practising lawyer. Prendergast believed in the sanctity of trial by jury and very seldom did he attempt to influence juries in their deliberations. He considered himself to be a guardian of the pluralist legalism of a mixed society.

Prendergast was born in Quebec City to James and Emile who soon recognized their son's quick mind and energy. His early schooling was at the Commercial Academy and Quebec Seminary. At Laval University he obtained his B.A. (1878) and his LL.B (1881). He soon moved to Winnipeg to practice law. With a mere seventeen votes he won the La Verandyre provincial seat for the Conservatives in 1886. He became the first Provincial Secretary in Premier Greenway's cabinet in 1888 when he switched to the Liberal Party, but he left one year later to become leader of the opposition. Prendergast, a staunch Catholic, left the government over its decision to abolish separate schools. Elected Mayor of St. Boniface in 1893 and 1896, he kept his legislative seat until 1897 when he was appointed Country Court Judge. He also served on the Board of Education of Manitoba from 1884 and 1890.

In 1902 Prendergast was appointed to the Supreme court of the North West Territories, succeeding C.B. Rouleau as the Catholic judge on the bench. Five years later he moved to the Supreme Court of Saskatchewan. From 1910 to 1922 he served on the Court of King's Bench of Manitoba, and later on its Court of Appeal. In 1930 he became Chief Justice of Manitoba.

Along the way, Prendergast served the University of Manitoba as Council member and earlier, the University of Saskatchewan as Senator. Earlier he was President of the Jean Baptiste Society of St. Boniface. The judge also wrote "amateur poetry" in his spare time.

Prendergast retired from the bench in 1944 and his busy life-in-the-law ended a year later.

RICHARD

After visiting the famous fort in Battleford, head eastward on your short drive on Highway #40 to Richard, named for a family that had an important "connection" with the early days at the fort.

EDOUARD RICHARD ((1844-1904)

Edouard Richard, the son of the Hon. Louis Richard and Hermine Prince, was educated at the College of Nicolet and McGill University, practised law with the future Prime Minister, Wilfred Laurier in Quebec's Athabaskaville, and served as Liberal Member of Parliament for Megantic from 1972 to 1878 before becoming Sheriff of the Northwest Territories. In 1886 he was named Inspector of Catholic Schools for the Battleford area. Proud of his Acadian heritage, Richard became a fine historian. His two- volume work on Acadia became a minor classic. In 1896 he was elected a Fellow of the Royal Society of Canada and was made Litt.D. of Laval University. In 1897 he was employed by the Canadian government to undertake historical research in Paris, France. He died in Battleford.

Richard was in charge of the December 20th, 1879 execution in Fort Saskatchewan of Swift Runner, a Cree cannibal who killed and devoured nine members of his family. The "purtiest hanging," as it was called, was first "arranged" by the RNWMP. Richard wrote: "I will, nevertheless, make bold to say that, as far as I may judge, my chief characteristic is kindness."

RICHARDSON

The settlement is a stone's throw south-east of Regina where Louis Riel was tried, sentenced and executed. Ponder the difference, if any, between legality and justice.

Would you have agreed with the Judge Hugh Richardson whose name adorns the settlement?

Do the locals know the connection with the nearby Davin community?

HUGH RICHARDSON (1826-1913)

The captured Louis Riel (1844-1885) was brought to Regina where he was imprisoned in the RNWMP barracks in a six and one-half foot by four and one-half foot cell and shackled with ball and chain. He prepared for his trial before Judge Hugh Richardson.

Of the eighty-four trials held in Battleford and Regina for participants in the 1885 Rebellion (Resistance), seventy-one were for treason-felony, twelve for murder, and only one, Riel's, for high treason. Richardson realized that the charge against Riel was under the medieval statute of 1352 which carried a mandatory death penalty.

The London-born lawyer, judge and chief justice of the NWT accepted the famous McNaghten rule: "A defence of insanity could be accepted only if it could be proved that the accused did not know the difference between right and wrong."

Richardson, it must be said, had considerable experience with the legal profession. In 1847 he was called to the bar of Upper Canada, practised at Woodstock until 1872 and served as crown attorney for part of that time. From 1872 to 1876 he was chief clerk of the Department of Justice at Ottawa, and then named stipendiary magistrate in the NWT, a member of the Territorial Executive Council, and legal advisor to the Lieutenant Governor. From 1887 to 1903 he served as chief justice of the NWT Supreme Court.

However, Richardson's role in Riel's May, 1885 trial was the "highlight" of his career. The quality and fairness of that trial continue to cause heated debate. The unilingual judge's charge to the jury was clearly biased against Riel.

The judge concluded by asking the jury to apply the McNaghten rules to Riel's case. On August 1st the jury returned a verdict of guilty and a recommendation for mercy. Nevertheless, Richardson passed the death sentence to the man who told the court: "Through the grace of God I am the founder of Manitoba."

Richardson's performance at the trial has been called "unimaginative if arguably fair." Other experts claim that the judge allowed Riel little opportunity for real justice. Was not an insane man put to death?

Hugh Richardson's pen was a mighty one. It pointed to the gallows which took the life of Louis Riel (patriot or traitor?) on November 16th, 1885.

Judge Richardson's last words to Louis Riel were: "It is now my painful duty to pass the sentence of the court upon you. And that is that you shall be taken now from here...[and] be taken to the place appointed for your execution, and there be hanged by the neck till you are dead. And may God have mercy on your soul."

In all, Richardson presided at the trial of seventy-two Cree allies, the "white rebels" Thomas Scott and William Jackson-as well as Riel. Richardson was often regarded as a punctual, imperturbable, patient man but perhaps biased against the Cree.

One story adds to Richardson's reputation. It happened that his daughter fell in love with a NWMP sub-constable and arranged to marry him secretly. Richardson found out almost immediately, had the groom arrested before the wedding night, and later he tried to coerce a jury to deliver a guilty verdict on four criminal charges he conferred on the policeman.

In 1902 Richardson retired after being passed over as the NWT's Chief Justice.

RIDPATH

After you reach Rosetown from the north east on Highway #7, make a studied examination of the community just west of the town. Watch for absent-minded professors, book-worms, and academic caps and gowns. Enjoy your conversations and debates: Enjoy the Ridpath enlightenment.

JOHN CLARK RIDPATH (1840-1900)

You would think that John was born with a pen in his hand. You would be taken by his forceful personality, impressive intelligence, remarkable vitality and admirable zeal for work. This man's memory combined with his love of learning and teaching made for a first class professor.

The farm boy from Putman County, Indiana received encouragement and instruction from his parents, Sally and Abraham. Only limited formal schooling was available for the boy. At age twenty-three he graduated from a nearby university founded by the Methodist Episcopal Church, started teaching, and later became principal and superintendent of schools. In 1869 he returned to his alma mater as professor of normal instruction and English literature. After later becoming professor of history and belles-letters, he became the university's vice-president. History was Ridpath's academic love. In 1882 he became professor of political philosophy and history.

Three years later he resigned from the university to devote himself exclusively to writing and publishing. However, he first put his powers of persuasion to work: Ridpath convinced the very wealthy Washington C. De Pau to become a patron of the Indiana institution. In 1884, Ridpath led the successful attempt to rename the institution DePau University.

Earlier, in 1875, he published his first book, *History of the United States, Prepared Especially for Schools*. His style was clear, direct and dramatic enough to capture reader's interest. He consistently held a high regard for fact and reliance on other authorities. His best known works include *A Popular History of the United States of America (1876)*, *Cyclopedia of Universal History* (4 vols. 1884-1885), and *Great Races of Mankind (4 vols.1880-1894)*. The productive writer was also editor-in-chief of *The Ridpath Library of Universal Literature* (25 vols. 1898). John Ridpath also wrote the biographies of President James A. Garfield, Prime Minister William E. Gladstone, among others.

Ridpath was also a happy family man. At age twenty-two he had married Hannah R. Smythe by whom he had five children. A full and useful life!

ROBINHOOD

If Robinhood got its name from the famous flour signs then where did that image originate? Ask the locals after you drive north from North Battleford on Highway #4. Stop first at Jackfish Lake, picnic, and practise your bow and arrow skills and then head for Robinhood. If you are robbed along the route, don't be overly concerned. Your money will be given to the poor.

ROBINHOOD

"The legendary hero of many English ballads, a rebel, an outlaw, the subject of movies, plays, poems, songs and tales", all refer to Robin Hood, known by millions of people world-wide. Some of those ballads date from the 14th Century or earlier. Those early ballads were the poetic expression of popular aspirations in northern England. That discontent led to the Peasant's Revolt of 1381. It can be said, therefore, if the earlier King Arthur was a noble's hero then Robin Hood was a people's hero.

Some claim that the outlaw hero lived as early as 1190 when there were many robbers, among whom were Robin Hood and Little John who lived in the woods where they robbed the rich and gave their gains to the poor. They would kill only when they were invaded. They would allow no woman to be molested.

Other sources tell us that the Sheriff of Nottingham was Robin's chief enemy. The rebel demanded hunting rights and often took "the King's deer." We are led to believe that Robin Hood's merry men were a constant bother to the authorities.

There are medieval ballads which mention the hero-outlaw: "Robin Hood and the Monk," "Lytyll Geste of Robin Hode," "Robin Hood and the Potter," "Robin Hood and the Guy of Gisborne." Post-medieval ballads add extras to the earlier ones-like "Maid Marian."

Hollywood, of course, has spread the appeal of Robin Hood's legend: Robin seldom missed with his well-aimed arrows. The handsome outlaw had a heart of gold. The king feared him. Women loved him. His men were merry. And on and on.

In spite of those descriptions, there still remain the intriguing questions: Was there an original, real Robin Hood? Or did someone pen a great lie?

RODDICK

Tour the battlegrounds of Batoche and Duck Lake, and then continue to the Roddick settlement a few canon shots to the north.

Arrive well scrubbed, please.

THOMAS RODDICK (1846-1923)

Britain's Joseph Lister (1827-1912) convinced his medical colleagues that far too many surgeries led to death by blood poisoning. Lack of cleanliness in the operating rooms was the problem. Lister proved that the sterilizing of dressings and instruments in carbolic acid would improve the situation. He usually sprayed his patients with a "light" acid solution before an operation. Heat sterilization of his instruments was part of his procedure.

Young Thomas Roddick of Harbour Grace, Newfoundland learned of Lister's work, and planned on a medical career for himself. Thomas attended school in Truro, Nova Scotia, and at age fourteen he became a doctor's assistant in that province. In 1869 he joined the Canadian militia and saw service two years later in a Fenian raid. The clever man was to become dean of medicine at McGill University, army medical officer in the 1885 Saskatchewan Resistance, and founder of the Medical Council of Canada in 1912.

Some of those wounded at Batoche, Duck Lake and Fish Creek were under Roddick's care in Saskatoon.

Surgeon Roddick led the fight for the creation of a system of common examinations throughout the provinces for those individuals seeking a licence to practise medicine. But he did more: He pioneered the Lister sterilization approach to surgery in Canada. Roddick was an LL.D of

Edinburgh University (1898), of Queen's (1903) and a D.Sc. of Oxford (1904).

Dr. Roddick served as a Conservative Member of Parliament for Montreal West from 1896-1904. For his services and excellence he was knighted in 1914. His persistence, and his careful research and writings had great impact. He inspired many Canadian surgeons to follow Lister's methods.

A sharp pen! A sharper scalpel.

ROULEAU

Travel south on Highway #6 from Regina for a few moments before turning west on Highway #714 to the community of Rouleau.

Is there a Canadian centre named for an individual who sentenced more people to death than did C.B. Rouleau? His pen made Rouleau part of Writers Corner.

CHARLES B. ROULEAU (1840-1901)

Rouleau was afraid for his life and that of his family so he made a bee-line to Swift Current. He was sure that the Indians were a threat to his home and other homes near Battleford.

On the night of April 23rd, 1885, Commander W.D. Otter's forces watched in frustration where from a few miles away they saw the night sky turn red-the "rebels" had burned down Judge Rouleau's home. His precious law books and family possessions, of course, were turned to ashes. Otter's forces relieved Battleford the next morning but found no enemy to fight. (Some of the men were to become jealous of Middleton's men at Batoche where the major fight took place.)

Judge Rouleau returned to Battleford. He had a job to do. He earlier told Lieutenant Governor Edgar Dewdney that "it is high time...Indians should be taught a severe lesson." That comment came from a man with limited experience of the situation.

Shortly after Riel's capture near Batoche, the trials for the allegedly guilty Metis and Indians began. Authorities agreed that to save money some trials should take place in Battleford.

So, on September 22nd, 1885, Wandering Spirit, described by the *Saskatchewan Herald* as "one of the greatest murderers that ever walked on two legs in America," was brought to trial before the Quebec-born Charles B. Rouleau, stipending magistrate. The prisoner, Big Bear's war chief, murderer of Agent Quinn, was a hurting man: Earlier he had attempted suicide by plunging a knife into his left lung.

The trial was over in a few minutes and Wandering Spirit was sentenced to be executed on November 27th. Indeed, eleven Indians (Later, three had their sentences changed to jail sentences.) were condemned to death in a seventeen day period. Still other Indians received long jail sentences for what many called "minor crimes" carried out during the 1885 Resistance. The prisoners did not have legal counsel. Some argue that Rouleau acted as both judge and jury.

Inside Fort Battleford's walls the scaffold was constructed. The ropes were tested. With wrists tied the eight condemned men climbed the steps, led by Deputy Sheriff A.P. Forget who carried the death warrants. Father Cochin, after whom nearby Cochin was later named, and Father Bignose followed. Nearly one hundred fifty armed police led by Major L. Crozier (who earlier lost the Duck Lake fight) ringed the three sides of the gallows. Some of the condemned men sang death chants. Others said their final words of regrets or defiance.

Eight nooses awaited the men who were placed in a single line. Their legs were firmly strapped at the ankles, veils were lowered, nooses were attached and adjusted, the priests prayed-and the bolt was withdrawn. All eight men fell. A sickening thud. The gallows strained from the weight, but held. After fifteen minutes a doctor, A.W. Rolph, pronounced them dead. Placed in rough coffins, the dead men were buried in a common grave near the fort.

Three days later, P.G. Laurie of the *Saskatchewan Herald* wrote: "It is devoutly to be hoped that the Indians at large will be duly impressed with the certainty with which punishment has overtaken their deluded fellows."

For nearly seven decades after that cold November day, the common grave remained uncared for and largely ignored. There are people today who remember seeing the bones of the dead becoming exposed caused by erosion. Some children fingered and played with those remains. Not until 1954 was the common grave covered with a concrete slab. A drooping single chain fence on short metal posts surrounded the rectangle.

Justice Rouleau became a member of the Board of Education of the Northwest Territories from 1885 to 1893. In 1887 he was appointed to the Supreme Court of the territories in the jurisdiction of Northern Alberta, a work he continued to his death.

Known to dislike aboriginals and being a strong advocate of capital punishment, the scholarly Rouleau wasted little time dispensing "justice." Rouleau did not have good relations with his colleagues on the bench. He also did not get along well with the ranching community. Rouleau once ruled that branding was inadmissible as evidence of ownership because, he believed, some people branded cattle that were not their property. It was the same judge who sentenced a Chinese man for an offense: "If I really thought you were guilty, I would give you ten years." He got two.

There is a famous photograph of Rouleau and other NWT justices including Hugh Richardson, the judge who sent Louis Riel to the gallows.

There are more than a few people who refer to Rouleau as "the hanging judge." Was justice or revenge involved? Or both? Justice Rouleau wielded a powerful pen.

RUNNYMEDE

Take Highway #5 east toward the Manitoba border. A few minutes past Kamsack you'll take that same highway south to Runnymede.

Be sure to picnic in a meadow.

Ask for John, the "reluctant" writer.

RUNNYMEDE (1215)

Most people know the story of "the brave men who forced King John" to sign the now famous Magna Charter of 1215. In the grassy meadow called Runnymede the king was forced to affix his seal on "the first great document in the 'Bible of English liberation.' " King John, some say, surpassed his predecessors in tyranny and wickedness. His course led to an open revolt of the barons of the realm.

In the main, the charter merely restated ancient liberties; but the closing provision expressly sanctioned rebellion against a king who should refuse to obey it. That is, it set laws of the land above the king's will. In the next two centuries, English monarchs were obliged to confirm the charter thirty-eight times. Its principles and some of its wording have passed into the constitution of American states and every Dominion. Some experts claim that the great charter established the principle of no taxation without the consent of the taxed.

[facsimile of Latin charter text]

Nullus liber homo capiatur, vel imprisonetur, aut dissaisiatur, aut utlagetur,
No free man shall be taken, or imprisoned, or dispossessed, or outlawed,

[facsimile of Latin charter text]

aut exuletur, aut aliquo modo destruatur, nec super eum ibimus nec super
or banished, or in any way destroyed, nor will we go upon him nor upon

[facsimile of Latin charter text]

eum mittemus, nisi per legale judicium parium suorum vel per legem terrae.
him send, except by the legal judgment of his peers or by the law of the land.

[facsimile of Latin charter text]

Nulli vendemus, nulli negabimus, aut differemus, rectum aut justiciam.
To no one will we sell, to no one will we deny, or delay, right or justice.

SECTIONS 39 AND 40 OF MAGNA CARTA.—The bars are facsimiles of the
writing in the charter, with the curious abbreviations of the medieval
Latin. Below each line is given the Latin in full with a translation.

The opening lines of the Magna Charter (sometimes spelled Carta) are as follows:

JOHN, by the grace of God, king of England, lord of Ireland,
duke of Normandy and Aquitaine, count of Anjou, to the
archbishops, bishops, abbots, earls, barons, justiciars,
foresters, sheriffs, reeves, servants, and all bailiffs and his
faithful people greeting. Know that by the suggestion of God
and for the good of our soul and those of all our predecessors
and of our heirs, to the honor of God and the exaltation of the
holy shurch, and the improvement of our kingdom, by the
advice of our venerable fathers Stephen, Archbishop of
Canterbury, primate of all England and Cardinal of the Holy
Roman Church....

The closing lines-after the listing of sixty-three articles-are as follows: "Witness the above named and many others. Given by the hand (King John's) in the meadow which is called Runnymede, between Windsor and Staines, on the fifteenth day of June, in the seventeenth year of our reign."

J.R. Green, British historian wrote:

'Foul as it is, hell itself is defiled by the fouler presence of John,' The terrible view of his contemporaries has passed into the sober judgement of history...John was the worst outcome of the Plantagenets. He united into one mass of wickedness their insolence, their selfishness, their unbridled lust, their cruelty and tyranny, their shamelessness, their superstition, their cynical indifference to honour or truth.

Equally damning are the comments of British clergyman, Bishop William Stubbs:

He was the very worst of all our kings: a man whom no oaths could bind, no pressure of conscience, no consideration of policy, restrain from evil; a faithless son, a treacherous brother, an ungrateful master; to his people a hated tyrant. Polluted with every crime that could disgrace a man, false to every obligation that should bind a king, he had lost half his inheritance by sloth, and ruined and desolated the rest.

RYERSON

After travelling east on Highway #1, you will reach Fleming near the Manitoba border. Turn south on Highway #600 to Maryfield. You are a stop away from the settlement once called Ryerson. Check the area for bookworms, enthused students and dedicated administrators—all deep in Writers Corner.

EGERTON RYERSON (1803-1882)

"Egerton Ryerson Founder of the School Systems of Ontario" is the inscription under the statue in front of Toronto's Ryerson Institute of Technology. It can be argued that "Founder of Western Canadian Education" should be added to that inscription.

The energetic Ryerson devoted his life to the establishment of "common schools" for all and leading that to a system of grammar (high) schools for those who might benefit from further study. His improvements were not unique: they were part of the mainstream of educational change taking place elsewhere in the western world. Sound schooling, he believed, could foster patriotism and loyalty, self-reliance, social cohesion, and tranquility. He believed that was the way Canada could become "the brightest gem in the crown of Her Britannic Majesty." Ryerson wanted public education (schooling) to be free, Christian, compulsory and universal.

Who was this man, the first prominent Ontario educator to be born in Canada? Born to a loyalist family on a farm near Victoria, Ryerson became attracted to Methodism. At age eighteen, he was ordered "out of the house" by his Tory Anglican father. He taught school for two years, suffered a nervous breakdown, entered the Methodist ministry by becoming a saddle-bag preacher.

In 1829 Ryerson was named first editor of the Methodist newspaper, the *Christian Guardian*. In print he criticized the stance of John Strachan, virtual "prime minister" of Upper Canada, and soon to be Archdeacon of York (Toronto). Strachan believed that the Church of England (Anglican) was the established church and therefore should gain exclusive claim to the income from the Clergy Reserves. (The 1791 Constitutional Act stated that one-seventh of the land be considered Clergy Reserves.) The issue was not settled until 1854 when the reserves were secularized.

Ryerson worked to establish Victoria College and become its first principal. Political considerations helped him become "second man" in the Canada West schools. Two years later he became chief superintendent. He was the right man for a tough job. When Ryerson made his famous study of European school systems, he visited more than twenty countries and brought back to Canada the best elements he had found. His trip and study resulted in his "Report of a System of Public Elementary Instruction for Upper Canada." It was his blueprint. For Ryerson, "Education is a public good; ignorance is a public evil." He added that an educated populace is "the best security for a good government and constitutional liberty." Education could be a vehicle to help people by the use of their reason to overcome ignorance, vice, juvenile delinquency and crime. That education, he claimed, must be a practical one.

The 1846 Common School Act implemented Ryerson's ideas: Centralized authority, common standards and grades. He encouraged Canadian texts (For some time he used the Irish National Series.) and materials. The Act also provided for a normal school. It also provided for a system of supervision and inspection.

Two years later he launched the *Journal of Education* which became a powerful force in publicizing his views on education. His superintendency, which lasted nearly a third of a century, remains significant to today: He got the public to accept the idea of a "free school"—supported by taxes from all citizens with property.

When Dr. Ryerson retired in 1876, he picked up his pen to write his *Story of My Life and a History of the Loyalists of America and Their Times.* The tireless Ryerson, it can be said, remains the most important English speaking individual to have contributed to Canadian school systems. A giant in the field of Canadian education. This giant stated with conviction:

-*Truly, circumstances alter cases, but circumstances do not change principles.*
-*Free and independent men in the legislature, as in the country, are the best counterpoise to faction and the main-spring of a nation's progress and greatness.*
-*Emigration to the United States is the fear of the hour. It is indeed going on to an extent truly alarming and astonishing.*

SERVICE

Service is a skip and a jump north-east of Carlyle in Writers Corner. Arrive in a rollicking mood, prepared to celebrate Canada's northernness-although you'll still be far from Service's beloved Klondike. Join your friends around the piano and lustily sing *The Shooting of Dan Mcgrew* as you "[come] out of the night, which was fifty below and into the din and the glare." Enjoy!

ROBERT SERVICE (1874-1958)

In his early years, Service worked as a gardener, a dishwasher, an orange-picker, a sandwich-maker and a sandhog. He often begged for food and accepted handouts from soup kitchens. He travelled with his guitar on which he played the verses he composed and sang. It was later that he went to the north and worked as a banker and composed the ballads for which he is famous.

Because of his rollicking ballads of the "frozen north", verse writer Robert Service has often been called "the Canadian Kipling." The poet, born in Preston, England, made his reputation in Canada which became his home in 1894, after wandering from California to British Columbia. For eight years he lived in the Yukon before becoming the *Toronto Star* correspondent during the 1912-1913 Balkan Wars. Service served in WW1 as an ambulance driver and war correspondent.

Perhaps Service's most popular poems are The *Shooting of Dan McGrew* and *The Cremation of Sam McGee*. His verse collections, the 1907 *Songs of a Sourdough* and the 1908 *Ballads of a Cheechako* were very popular. Service's 1910 *The Trail of '98* is a moving novel of men and conditions in the Klondike.

His later volumes of verse, the 1916 *Rhymes of a Red Cross Man* and the 1940 *Bar Room Ballads* were also well-received. His autobiographical works, the 1945 *Ploughman of the Moon* and the 1948 *Harper of Heaven* are less well known.

The Law of the Yukon illustrates the pungency of Service's poetry:

> *This is the law of the Yukon, and she ever makes*
> *it plain;*
> *Send not your foolish and feeble; send me your*
> *strong and your sane...*
> *Send me the best of your breeding; lend me your*
> *chosen ones;*
> *Them I will take to my bosom, them will I call*
> *my sons;*
> *Them I will gild with my treasure, them will I*
> *glut with my meat;*
> *But the others-the misfits, the failures, I trample*
> *under my feet....*

Perhaps *The Shooting of Dan McGrew* best shows the rollicking nature of Service's poetry:

> *A bunch of the boys were whooping it up in the*
> *Malamute saloon;*
> *The kid that handles the music box was hitting a*
> *rag-time tune;*
> *Back of the bar in a poker game, sat Dangerous*
> *Dan McGrew,*
> *And watching his luck was his light-o-love, the*
> *lady that's known as Lou....*

Just as famous was *The Cremation of Sam McGee*:

> *THERE are strange things done in the midnight sun*
> *By the men who moil for gold;*
> *The Arctic trails have their secret tales*
> *That would make your blood run cold;*
> *The Northern Lights have seen queer sights,*
> *But the queerest they ever did see*
> *Was the night on the marge of Lake Lebarge*
> *I cremated Sam McGee...*

One wonders how many youths have been inspired by Service to become members of a police force. Consider *Clancy of the Mounted Police:*

In the little Crimson Manual-it's written plain
and clear
That who would wear the scarlet coat shall say
goodbye to fear;
Shall be a guardian of the right, a sleuth-hound
of the trail-
In the little Crimson manual, there's no such word
as "fail"...
It's duty, duty, first and last, the Crimson
Manual saith;
The Scarlet Rider makes reply: "It's duty-to
the death."...

The vagabond-turned writer, the poet of the Yukon, remains one of Canada's most loved and quoted poets.

SOUTHEY

Drive thirty minutes north of Regina on Highway #6. Southey awaits you. Note some of the street signs: Frost, Cowper, Burns, Byron and Browning. The "main drag" is called Keats. Ask the locals if Mr. Southey equalled the talent exhibited by those five individuals.

ROBERT SOUTHEY (1774-1818)

The Bristol-born poet, letter writer, prose and drama writer to this day stays in the shadows of his literary contemporaries, Wordsworth and Coleridge. The son of a dry-goods merchant was expelled from London's Westminister School for criticizing, in a school magazine, the excessive whippings of his fellow students. Without doubt the expulsion roused the rebellious side of his personality and confirmed his enthusiasm for what he called the "ideals" of the French Revolution.

When Southey entered Oxford university (he left without a degree) he wrote the long poem *Joan of Arc* which tells of his support for the French Revolution. At Oxford he learned a bit about boating and swimming but little else. He and Coleridge planned an ideal colony in Pennsylvania. The plan did not materialize so Southey turned to law. He disliked that calling so he turned to poetry.

In 1795 Southey secretly married Edith Fricker, whose sister, Sara, he encouraged Coleridge to marry. Later that year he travelled to Portugal and Spain to study their literature.

He shared a house with Coleridge at Keswick in England's Lake District where the two joined with Wordsworth to form the well-known "Lake School" of poetry. Contrary to his own belief, Southey was not nearly as gifted as his two companions. In order to live, he did a great deal of hack writing, wrote a number of long narrative poems, and penned several biographies including the life of Lord Nelson.

In spite of his lesser talent, in 1813 he was appointed Poet Laureate thanks to the influence of Sir Walter Scott (the politics of poetry!), who recognized the ease and clarity of Southey's poetry. The position provided him with a government pension.

The renegade's poetry is little read today. However, a few of his lyrics and ballads-e.g. *Battle of Blenheim*- are valued. Irony and terseness best describe the work. In that poem is his subtle comment on the futility of war:

> *"But what good came of it at last?"*
> *Quoth little Peterkin.*
> *"Why I cannot tell," said he,*
> *"But, 'twas a famous victory."*

Robert Southey was proud of his industriousness and work habits. After telling a lady that he regularly started work at six A.M. and finished at bedtime, she brilliantly asked: "And pray, friend, when dost thou think?"

In spite of criticisms Southey wrote *The Cataract of Lodore* which is one of the best examples of sustained onomatopoeia in the English language. He describes the cataract:

...Collecting, projecting.
Receding and speeding,
And shocking and rocking,
And darting and parting,
And threading and spreading,
And whizzing and hissing,
And dripping and skipping,
And hitting and splitting,
And shining and twining,
And rattling and battling,
And shaking and quaking,
And pouring and roaring,
And waving and raving,
And tossing and crossing,
And flowing and going,
And running and stunning,
And foaming and roaming,
And dinning and spinning,
And dropping and hopping,
And working and jerking,
And guggling and struggling,
And heaving and cleaving,
And moaning and groaning,
And glittering and frittering,
And gathering and feathering,
And whitening and brightening,
And quivering and shivering,
And hurrying and scurrying,
And thundering and floundering....

Southey had his strong opinions. Consider what he said about the famous poet Percy Blysse Shelley: "He was a liar and a cheat; he paid no regard to truth, nor to any kind of moral obligation."

Robert Southey: Clever but no genius? Perhaps. Observe his quotes:

-*The pander of posterity.*
-*Your true lover of literature is never fastidious.*
-*A vague, a dizzy, a tumultuous joy.*
-*We wage no war with women nor with priests.*
-*Blue, darkly, deeply, beautifully blue.*
-*The Monk my son, and my daughter the nun.*
-*Oh! What blockheads are those wise persons who think it is necessary that a child should comprehend everything he reads.*
-*My name is Death; the last best friend am I.*
-*Live as long as you may, the first twenty years of your life are the longest half of your life.*
-*Beware of those who are homeless by choice.*

Perhaps British writer Thomas Love Peacock says it loudest: "Mr. Southey wades through ponderous volumes of travels and old chronicles, from which he carefully selects all that is false, useless and absurd, as being essentially poetical; and when he has a commonplace book full of monstrosities, strings them into an epic."

SWINBOURNE

Someone made a spelling error by adding an "o" to A.C. Swinburn's name. Would a poet-writer be well-pleased to learn that his name was so misspelled?

Take Highway #14 from Saskatoon to Unity, have lunch and proceed a little west to the Swinbourne settlement.

ALGERNON CHARLES SWINBURNE (1837-1909)

Swinburne came from a distinguished family: His mother was the daughter of an Earl and his father was an Admiral. He was educated at Eton and Oxford (he left in 1860 without a degree) where he became familiar with ancient and Roman languages.

The young man cut a wide swath. Yet Swinburne, with his small elf-like body, crowned with a shock of bright red hair, was a nervous, frail man who never forgot the bullying he received when a boy. He travelled through Europe before settling in London where he spent much time with writers and artists of the day. Before long, he gained a reputation as a fine poet and literary critic. His first major success came with the verse drama *Atalanta in Calydn*. (1865) He followed with a series of poems and ballads which clearly show his preoccupation with paganism, masochism and flagellation. As the years passed, he fell deeper and deeper into acute alcoholism. His defiance of conventional sexual morality made him a scandalous figure in Victorian England. (*Punch* magazine called him Swine-born.) The keen flagellant had a liaison with a rather plump, middle-aged American circus rider who complained that "I can't make him understand that biting's no good."

In 1867 Swinburne met his idol, Giuseppi Mazzini, the Italian patriot who greatly influenced the poet's opinions and work. He had long been influenced by the Greek classics as well.

By 1879 the man was incapable of managing his own life. His alcoholism and "other excesses" led to his collapse. Theodore Watt-Dunton took charge and "cured and cared" for Swinburne for the next thirty years. Without that help and organization Swinburne might well have written nothing. So the gifted Swinburne produced a stream of books, twenty-three volumes of poetry, prose and drama.

Swinburne was also an important and prolific literary critic. Well known are his monographs on Shakespeare, Hugo, Dickens, Blake, Shelley, among others. Listen as he flogged Walt Whitman (1819-1892), the American poet:

> Under the dirty clumsy paws of a harper whose plectrum is a muck-take, any tune will become a chaos of discords. ...Mr. Whitman's Eve is a drunken apple-woman, indecently sprawling in the slush and garbage of the gutter amid the rotten refuse of her overturned fruit-stall: but Mr. Whitman's Venus is a Hottentot wench under the influence of cantharides and adulterated sun.

He went on to degrade American writer Ralph Waldo Emerson:

> A gap-toothed and hoary-headed ape...who now in his doteage spits and chatters from a dirtier perch of his own finding and fouling: coryphaeus or choragus of his Bulgarian tribe of autocoprophagous baboons....

He described the American authoress Harriet Beecher Stowe as "a blatant Bassarid of Boston, a rampant Maenad of Massachusetts." The man had disgust for both Carlyles when he referred to them as "that very sorry pair of phenomena, Thomas Cloakina and his Goody."

The "easy-living" Swinburne called fellow poet Shelley "the most affected of sensualists and the most pretentious of profilgates."

Swinburne has his detractors too. American essayist and poet Ralph Waldo Emerson (1803-1882) commented in an interview in *Leslie's Illustrated Newspaper* (January 3rd, 1874): "[Swinburne is] a perfect leper and a mere sodomite, which criticism recalls Carlyle's scathing description of that poet-as a man standing in a cesspool and adding to its contents."

Many readers are impressed by the luscious quality of his literary style. His enthusiasm for liberty, his sensitiveness to beauty and his love for "the noble art of praising" all shine clearly in his work. Nevertheless, the man remains the enfant terrible of Victorian poetry in spite of his seldom-equated master of melodious verse. Consider these verses of *The Match*:

> *If love were what a rose is,*
> *And I were like the leaf,*
> *Our lives would grow together*
> *In sad or singing weather*
> *Blown fields or flowerful closes,*
>   *Green pleasure or grey grief;*
> *If love were what the rose is,*
> *And I were like the leaf.*
>
> *If I were what the words are,*
>   *And love were like the tune,*
> *With double sound and single*
> *Delight our lips would mingle,*
> *With kisses glad as birds are*
>   *That get sweet rain at noon;*
> *If I were what the words are,*
>   *And love were like the tune...*
> *If you were queen of pleasure*
>   *And I were king of pain,*
> *We'd hunt down love together,*
> *Pluck out his flying-feather,*
> *And teach his feet a measure,*
>   *And find his mouth a rein;*
> *If you were queen of pleasure,*
>   *And I were king of pain.*

Some experts consider that the last six stanzas of his *Garden of Persephone* to be the most musical in the English language.

There is a story involving the head boy at Eton who told the other lads to think about the little red-haired Swinburne: "If even you see that boy, kick him-and if you are too far off to kick him, throw a stone...." One can only wonder how that bullying affected that troubled youth. If you were to make a movie called "Swinburne" who would you choose to play the leading role?

More Swinburne quotes:
-Man, a dunce uncouth, errs in age and youth: babies know the truth.
-When fate has allowed to any man more than one great gift, accident or necessity seems usually to contrive that one shall encumber and impede the other.
-Fiddle, we know, is diddle: and diddle, we take it, is dee.
-If you were queen of pleasure,
And I were the king of pain.
-For no man under the sky lives twice, outliving his day.
-Sweet red splendid kissing mouth.
-In heaven, if I cry to you then, will you hear or know?
-But god, if a God there be, is the substance of men which is man.
-Green leaves of thy labour, white flowers of thy thought, and red fruit of thy death.
-Superflux of pain.

Swinburne was as "kinky" as they come.

TANNAHILL

Perhaps your trip should take place on Burns Night, January 25th. Then you and Robert Tannahill will both have honoured the Scottish bard. Why don't you honour Tannahill as well?

Drive west on the Trans-Canada (#1 Highway) and turn south to Maple Creek. Turn a bit east and by the time your haggis cools you'll be in the settlement called Tannahill. Avoid canals.

ROBERT TANNAHILL (1774-1810)

By eight in the morning most of the townspeople had learned that the young man had committed suicide by drowning in the canal. The poet's silver watch and coat had been left on the south side of the culvert. Two of Glasgow's newspapers on Monday, May 21st, 1819 printed the following: "Thursday morning a young man was found lying in the Cart a little above Paisley. Some of his clothes were found near the spot, which led to the discovery of the melancholy circumstance."

What was the history of the flautist, poet, songwriter Robert Tannahill which led to his sad ending?

Robert, the fifth child and fourth son of a successful Scottish weaver from Paisley, was to experience years of physical weakness and later considerable mental illness. During his earliest years he was in considerable pain: he had a delicate constitution. The infant had a bent right foot, which was later straightened. He didn't distinguish himself in school but he did entertain his friends by making up poems about people of the town. He taught himself to play the flute with fine skill.

At age twelve Robert left school to become an apprentice with his father's weaving trade-a five year arrangement. The boy loved walking to strengthen his legs and body but exertion caused him pain. He had companionship with his four brothers, all in the weaving trade.

The young Tannahill read the poetry of Robbie Burns (1759-1796) and was so enthused that he took long walks through "Burns Country." Encouraged to write, he kept an ink bottle and pen next to his loom.

He met Jenny Tennant with whom he kept company for three years. For reasons unknown the couple quarrelled and the romance was finished. Perhaps due to his failed romance and an economic downturn the twenty-six year old Robert moved to Bolton, England where for two years he practiced his weaver's trade.

Robert was called home because his father was dying. He then settled in his mother's house and continued his weaving and writing. When he asked his friends to review his writing he became morose and sullen because of any negative comments.

A few people scorned the slender, mild-looking writer, his features somewhat feminine. He was only five foot four, had a rather long nose, small mouth, thin lips, and soft, mild grey eyes. His dry cough rasping in his breast was bothersome to some people. He wrote the following lines which described his health:

> But, ere a few short summers gae,
> Your friend will mix his kindred clay;
> For fell Disease tugs at my breast
> To hurry me away.

It might be added that Robert and all other members of his literary club were heavy smokers. His own teeth were blackened. Tannahill wrote about the club:

> Encircled in a cloud of smoke
> Sat the convivial core;
> Like lightning flash'd the merry joke,
> The thundering laugh did roar.

Tannahill was a founder of one of the world's first Burns' Club. Two of the first toasts proposed were: "May Burns be admired while thistle grows in Caledonia" and "May the genius of Scotland be as conspicuous as her mountains."

The weaver-poet sent scores of poems and songs to respectable periodicals of the day. Many were published. In a letter Robert spoke of how pleasant it was to hear his songs being sung: "Perhaps the highest pleasure ever I derived from those things has been the hearing, as I walked down the pavement at night, a girl within doors rattling away at some of them."

The temperate, industrious Tannahill had a fine way with words. Consider *The Storm*-the first two verses:

> Now the dark rains of Autumn discolour the brook,
> And the rough winds of Winter the woodlands deform;
> Here, lonely, I lean by the sheltering rock,
> Listening to the voice of the loud howling storm.

How dreadfully furious it roars on the hill,
The deep groaning oaks seem all writhing with pain.
Now awfully calm, for a moment 'tis still,
Then bursting it howls and it thunders again.

On a spring day 1810, Tannahill walked to nearby Glasgow. He arrived terribly tired and incoherent. His physical and mental problems were too much for him. At about three in the morning he quietly left a relative's house and headed for the canal.

Tannahill's grave can be found at the Canal Street cemetery. In 1866 a monument was erected over his grave. Some of his works remain popular today – *The Braes o' Balquhidder, Braes o' Gleniffer, O are ye Sleepin' Maggie, and Jessie the Flower o' Dunblaine.*

A complex man with a talented pen.

THACKERAY

Leave Saskatoon and drive west on Highway #14 through Biggar and Wilkie to the community called Thackeray. Ask the locals if they know Becky Sharp. It is likely the area was named after Becky's creator.

WILLIAM MAKEPEACE THACKERAY (1811-1863)

William was born in India where his father well served the East India Company. When the son was five, his father died. The lad was sent to England to be reared by an aunt who enrolled him in the famous Charterhouse School. There he had his nose badly broken in a fight; the crooked beak was never straightened.

The youth tried Cambridge University but did not take a degree. He then toured the continent, tried law and journalism. While in a Parisian art school he met and married a penniless Irish girl, Isabella Shawe. The Thackerays had three daughters before Isabella's "mental derangement" ended the marriage.

His successful work as a journalist, especially with *Punch*, encouraged him to become a full-time writer.

At age thirty-seven, Thackeray published the novel, *Vanity Fair,* which brought him swift popularity especially among the "upper classes' in spite of the fact it satirized them. His novel describes the roles of the scheming woman, Becky Sharp-even though he was an upper class snob and critic! Pretence, snobbery, pomposity and sham among others angered the writer. (He claimed, "every person who manages another is a hypocrite.") He followed that success with *Pendennis* and H*enry Esmond,* a story about the reign of Queen Anne, and considered to be one of the best historical novels in the English language.

Thackeray became a public lecturer and made two lecture tours to the United States. His book, The Virginians was set partly there. He created a rather favourable picture of the American south.

The somewhat bitter humourist was once asked about his smoking habit. He replied: "The pipe draws wisdom from the lips of the philosopher and shuts up the mouth of the foolish." However, friends considered Thackeray to be a kind, loveable and open-minded individual. He was an impressive, tall man with a large head and "a big body to match."

Thackeray became a candidate for parliament but was defeated.

The gifted writer also wrote verse and entertaining ballads. It seems that his hard work and long hours led to his bad health. Two days before Christmas, 1863, Thackeray died in spite of the devoted care of his daughters. A commemorative bust of him was placed in Westminister Abbey.

The author blackballed a man proposed for membership in London's Garrick Club: "I blackballed him because he is a liar [and] he calls himself ill when he isn't." At that club, Thackeray was confronted by a pompous Guards officer who teased the writer because he was going to have his portrait painted. "Full-length?" asked the officer. Thackeray replied: "No, full-length portraits are for soldiers, so we can see their spurs. With authors, the other end of the man is the principal thing."

His bitter pen offered this negative assessment of American lack of grace: "I saw five of them at supper...the other night with their knives down their throats. It was awful." Criticism flew both ways. British art critic and author John Ruskin commented: "Thackeray settled like a meat-fly on whatever one had for dinner; and made one sick of it."

However, as the following Thackeray statement suggests, the writer also had his moments of self-deprecation: "Even when I am reading my lectures I often think to myself, 'what a humbug you are', and I wonder the people don't find it out." He was the same man who said "I never know whether to pity or congratulate a man on coming to his senses."

Thackeray: A big man with a sharp pen! Observe:

-He who meanly admires mean things is a Snob.
-It is impossible, in our condition of Society, not to be sometimes a Snob.
-We love being in love, that's the truth on't.
-Nothing like blood, sir, in hosses, dawgs, and men.
-'Tis strange what a man may do, and the woman yet think him an angel.
-Why do they always put mud into coffee on board steamers? Why does the tea generally taste of boiled boots?

-*When I say that I know women, I mean that I know that I don't know them. Every single woman I ever knew is a puzzle to me, as, I have no doubt, she is to herself.*
-*Remember, it is as easy to marry a rich woman as a poor woman.*
-*There are some meannesses which are too mean even for a man-woman, lovely woman alone, can venture to commit them.*
-*If a man's character is to be abused...there is nobody like a relation to do the business.*

TROSSACHS, ESK and ROBSART

To set the mood properly, you might wish to ride your favourite steed (reasons to follow) to Trossachs on Highway #18, a bit west of Weyburn. The centre is not named after a writer but is honoured for a place found in the prose and poetry of Walter Scott. Shouldn't Trossachs be considered part of Writers Corner?

One of Scott's long poems, *Marmion*, features Lochinvar, a young knight who "swam the Eske River where ford there was none." From Saskatoon, take Highway #16 to Lanigan and on to Esk-named in honour of the Eske River. Scott's Kennilworth, set in Elizabethan England, is considered one of the finest historical novels which features a tangled web of betrayals and lies. Amy Robsart, after whom Robert was named, is the heroine of the story. Amy suffers a cruel ending.

Follow the famed Red Coat Trail (Highway #13) south west from Shaunavon to Robsart. Bring Scott's novel with you. Get out your lawn chair and enjoy southwestern Saskatchewan's magnificent sky.

Think about poor Amy.

WALTER SCOTT (1771-1832)

Many experts consider Walter Scott to be the inventor and greatest practitioner of the historical novel. The son of an Edinburgh lawyer suffered from infantile paralysis as a child, and was sent to the country where he was cared for by an aunt. She told him romantic tales and read to him from the stirring ballads and legends of the Border Wars. When Scott was a little older he wandered the border areas learning the legends as told by the peasants he met. Those stories inspired his later writing. Scott attended the University of Edinburgh, studied law, became a sheriff but continued to be a voracious reader of history, drama, poetry, romances and fairy tales.

It was not until he was forty-three years old that he began his career as a novelist. After that, much of his work was done to get rid of his debts. He spent his fortune and the labours of his last years, often in pain, clearing up those obligations. He died peacefully but lamented and admired. "The prince of romances" conquered the world with his historical novels. In addition, he has been called "the sweetest singing poet."

A fine example of Scott's genius is found in *The Lady of the Lake* which notes Trossachs (as does his 1818 *Rob Roy*). Part of the poem describes the riding hunters, their dogs and the stag they were pursuing for the kill. Consider:

The stag at eve had drunk his fill,
Where danced the moon on Monan's rill,
And deep his midnight lair had made
But, when the sun his beacon red
Had kindled on Benvoirlich's head,
The deep-mouthed bloodhound's heavy bay
Resounded up the rocky way...

For twice that day, from shore to shore,
The gallant stag swam stoutly o'er...

The wily quarry shunned the shock,
And turned him from the opposing rock;
Then, dashing down a darsome glen,
Soon lost to hound and hunter's ken,
In deep Trossach's wildest nook
His solitary refuge took...

Then through the dell his horn resounds,
From vain pursuit to call the hounds.
Back limped, with slow and crippled pace,
The sulky leaders of the chase....

The generous, kindly, lover-of-all-mankind is, perhaps, better known for his 1820 Ivanhoe which treats England in the Age of Richard Coeur-de-Lion. That year he was made a baronet. His literary conquest had brought Scott wealth and world fame such as no writer before him had enjoyed. The story teller was a master of dialogue. As mentioned, he lost most of his fortune.

There is a famous account of Walter Scott and Lady Scott who passed a field of playful lambs. "No wonder that poets from the past have made lambs the symbols of peace and innocence," noted the writer. His wife replied" Delightful creatures indeed, especially with mint sauce."

Scott, however, often had the last word. When William Wordsworth said that he had great contempt for Aristotle, Scott responded: "But not, I take it, that contempt which familiarity breeds."

The writer who gave Trossachs and Esk their names showed wit and quick thinking even as a boy in school. There he noted that his debating opponent while talking often fumbled and fiddled with a particular vest button. So, secretly, Scott took a pair of scissors and snipped off the boy's button. During the forthcoming debate the opponent reached for the button, became upset, stuttered and then fell silent. A victory for young Scott.

In spite of Scott's successes, the British essayist William Hazlett commented: "Sir Walter Scott (when all is said and done) is an inspired butler." A minority report. Some of Scott's interesting quotes follow:

- *- Breathes there the man, with soul so dead,*
Who never to himself hath said,
This is my own, my native land.
-Steady of heart, and stout of hand.
-November's sky is chill and drear,
November's leaf is red and sear.
-To lead but one measure, drink one cup of wine.
-The ancient and now forgotten pastime of high jinks.
-'Pax vobiscum' will answer all queries.
-Fair, fat and forty.
-The blockheads talk of my being like Shakespeare-
not fit to tie his brogues.
-For love will still be lord of all.
-O what a tangled web we weave,
When first we practise to deceive.
-Music is the universal language of mankind.

TWAIN

Take a thirty minute drive east from Swift Current on the Trans Canada Highway. Before you reach Herbert you will be in the Twain community, likely named in honour of the humourist, Mark Twain.

If you meet three boys named Tom, Huck and Jim, sit for a spell and be entertained. Tom might entice you to whitewash his fence.

MARK TWAIN (1835-1910)

Samuel Langhorne Clemens grew up in Hannibal, Missouri on the Mississippi's west bank. At age eleven he became a full-time apprentice to a local printer. Later he became a compositor for his brother's newspaper, The

Hannibal Journal, and then he worked as an itinerant printer. Clemens became an apprentice to a steamboat pilot, and in 1859 he received his pilot's licence. Steamboat travel on the Mississippi was curtailed by the American Civil War 1861-1865.

Clemens joined his brother in an 1861 trip to the Nevada Territory where Samuel became a writer for the *Virginia City Territorial Enterprise.* Clemens then took the pseudonym Mark Twain-a river man's term for "two fathoms deep"-and thus just barely enough for navigation. Three years later he moved to California where his reputation as a writer was established. While at a mining camp he heard and then wrote the famous *The Celebrated Jumping Frog of Calaveras County.*

In 1866 Twain visited Hawaii as a correspondent for *The Sacramento Union,* publishing accounts of his trip and later giving popular lectures. Later world tours took place leading to more of his writing and lecturing.

In 1876 Twain published *Tom Sawyer,* a narrative of boyish escapades. His next novel, *Huckelberry Finn* is considered by many as his finest and an American masterpiece of literature. (Ernest Hemingway once said that all American literature begins with this book.) In 1889 he published *A Connecticut Yankee in King Arthur's Court* in which a Yankee is transplanted back in time to medieval Britain. Other titles and lectures followed.

The humourist, writer and lecturer had many difficulties. He made poor investments, often lacked sufficient funds, and suffered the death of his wife, Olivia Langdon (married in 1870) and two daughters. For some years the family lived in Hartford, Connecticut before settling in Florence, Italy.

Bitter pessimism and mordant humour are found especially in Twain's later works. The cigar smoker always claimed it was easy to quit: "I've done it a hundred times." "In a world without women," Twain was asked, "what would

men become?"Twain answered: "Scarce, sir. Mighty scarce."
Some of his memorable quotes are:

-*The weakest of all weak things is virtue that has not
been tested in the fire.*
-*Reader, suppose you were an idiot; and suppose you
were a member of Congress; but I repeat myself.*
-*Man is the only animal that blushes. Or needs to.*
-*If you pick up a starving dog and make him
prosperous, he will not bite you. That is the principal
difference between a dog and a man.*
-*When some men discharge an obligation, you can hear
the report for miles around.*
-*If man had created man, he would be ashamed of his
performance.*
-*Fleas can be taught nearly anything that a
Congressman can.*
-*In the first place God made idiots; this was for practice;
then he made school boards.*
-*Why do you sit there looking like an envelope without
any address on it?*
-*Cauliflower is nothing but cabbage with a college
education.*
-*Wagner's music is better than it sounds.*
-*The criric's symbol should be the tumble-bug; he
deposits his egg on somebody else's dung, otherwise
he could not hatch it.*
-*It could possibly be shown by facts and figures that
there is no distinctively native American criminal class
except Congress.*
-*I am not an editor of a newspaper and shall always try
to do right and be good so that God will not make me
one.*
-*This is the first time I was ever in a city where you
couldn't throw a brick without breaking a church
window. (Montreal)*
-*Kings is mostly rapscallions.*
-*Such is the human race. Often it does seem a pity
that Noah and his party didn't miss the boat.*
-*The [newspaper] reports of my death are greatly
exaggerated.*

On a train Twain bragged to a fellow passenger that he had caught a hundred pounds of the finest bass one could ever hope to see. When Twain found out that his listener was a game warden he quickly added: "I'm the biggest damned liar in the United States." On another occasion, Twain swore violently after he cut himself shaving. His wife attempted to shame him by repeating his words. Twain responded: "You have the words, my dear, but I'm afraid you'll never master the tune."

Twain's wit usually came out on top. When the humourist once fingered a painting by Whistler the famed artist shouted: "Can't you see it isn't dry yet?" Twain replied: "Oh, I don't mind. I have my gloves on."

Further wit showed when he observed, "An ethical man is a Christian holding four aces." And he advised, "When angry count four; when very angry, swear!"

Halley's comet appeared the year Twain was born and returned the year he died. Those appearances bracketed the life of a gifted human being.

The American writer William Faulkner had a more critical view of Twain's ability: "[Twain was] a hack writer who would not have been considered a fourth rate in Europe as he tricked out a few of the old proven sure fire literary skeletons with sufficient local color to intrigue the superficial and the lazy." A minority report!

VALJEAN

Leave Moose Jaw west on the Trans-Canada Highway to Chaplin. Stop. You have passed the settlement, Valjean, likely named after the literary figure created by the pen of Victor Marie Hugo.

VICTOR HUGO (1802-1885)

In print and on stage and screen, Victor Hugo's *Les Miserables* has entertained and enlightened millions of people worldwide. The author's intent was to show the threefold problem of his century: the destruction of children, the degradation of proletarian man, and the fall of woman through hunger and hopelessness. The characters Jean Valjean and the waif, Gavroche, among others, won Hugo a vast readership. The 1862 publication was a love story and a mystery. Social injustice was the core of the story.

Who was this man, Hugo, whose pen produced poems, plays, novels, satires, dramas, epics and on and on-not to exclude the novel, *Notre Dame de Paris* (1830)? There we read about Quasimodo, the hunchback, Esmeralda, the gypsy girl, Frollo the archdeacon, and the others. Yes, who was this man with a vision of mystical grandeur, remarkable versatility and breadth of creation?

The erratically schooled Hugo experienced a nomadic early life. He began his serious writing when an adolescent because he wanted "to escape the ordinary life." In 1822 he married his childhood sweetheart, Adele Foucher, with whom he had four children. He celebrated his love for Adele in posting his first signed book in which he wrote: "Poetry is the most intimate of all things." Hugo, the romanticist, used Shakespeare, the Bible, and Homer as his chief sources. He and other young writers found richness and beauty in the Medieval Period.

Often his immense egoism (Ego Hugo was his motto) and his deep melancholy bothered his family and friends. Tormented by what he considered his wife's coldness-and by his inordinate sexual cravings-Hugo fell in love with a young actress, Juliette Drovet, who lived in his shadow for fifty years. When he was eighty, one of his grandsons surprised him in the arms of a young laundress. The very cool Hugo announced: "Look Little George, this is what they call genius."

Hugo's changing political beliefs brought him to the English Channel Islands, Guernsey and Jersey, where he experienced the supernatural. Under the influence of a female voyante he believed he communicated with the spirits of Shakespeare, Racine, Dante and even Jesus. The séance that affected him most was the "visit" he had with his daughter who had drowned years earlier. Juliette stayed loyal to him during the seventeen years he was away from the mainland. His wife had left him earlier. Hugo's mysticism and belief in reincarnation affected his life and his relationships.

Initially Hugo supported Napoleon III who was later removed after France's defeat in the Franco-Prussian War. Hugo wrote: "Because we have had a Great Napoleon we must now have a Little One?" So Hugo returned to Paris.

If Hugo found life to be a struggle, an unfair struggle, then that sentiment is surely found in the character Jean Valjean, one of literature's great creations.

How many people have known injustices such as were experienced by the "convict" Jean Valjean? Hugo had many observations worth reading:

-I am for religion against religions.
-The sewer is the conscience of the city.
-Who stops revolution half way? The bourgeoisie.
-God made himself man: granted. The Devil made himself woman.
-An invasion of armies can be resisted; an invasion of ideas cannot be resisted.
-A fixed idea ends in madness or heroism.
-Envy is an admission of inferiority.
-And now, Lord God, let us explain ourselves to each other.
-We are all under the sentence of death, but with a sort of indefinite reprieve.
-If we must suffer, let us suffer nobly.
-Adversity makes men, and prosperity makes monsters.
-God made only water, but man made wine.

WOLLASTON LAKE

Why don't you rent a small aircraft in Prince Albert, fly north and stop at La Ronge for supplies and fuel. Head out north, north-east, past the fifty eighth and enjoy the beauty of the one-hundred-thousand lakes of Northern Saskatchewan. A pleasant airstrip awaits you on the east side of Wollaston Lake. If you flew low you would spot the wild life and the raw beauty of one of the unspoiled areas of the world. When you arrive, you may want to search for a platinum source.

WILLIAM HYDE WOLLASTON   (1766-1828)

Here is a case of a successful doctor turning to a different career in chemistry and related sciences. Young William did well in London's Charterhouse school and later in Cambridge University. He practised medicine after his 1793 graduation. He was elected a Fellow of the Royal Society that year and later served a long time as its secretary.

Soon after leaving medicine in 1800, Wollaston became partially blind. That difficulty did not stop his pioneer work in the field of chemistry. In 1804 he discovered how to work platinum in a practical manner. His secret process netted him a fortune of £30,000. He was the first to detect the metals rhodium and palladium in crude platinum. Wollaston investigated voltaic cells and showed that they generated static electricity, thus demonstrating that the frictional and current electricity are identical.

Scientist Wollaston supported Dalton's atomic theory, studied the theory of multiple proportions in chemistry, placed crystallography on a firm quantative base, worked with ultraviolet rays, studied optics, and examined many metals. It is clear, however, that his method of making platinum malleable was his most famous accomplishment.

Wollaston, among others, opposed the adoption of the decimal system of weights and measures. He favoured the use of the imperial gallon measure which parliament adopted in 1824. His wealth allowed him to establish a fund in the Geological Society of London. The famed Wollaston prize resulted.

The mineral wollastonite was named after him.

WORDSWORTH

Your last stop in Writers Corner should be Wordsworth. The greatness of William Wordsworth's writing demands it. (Residents of nearby Carlyle might well insist that their man, Thomas Carlyle, deserves the honour.) Take the short drive from Carlyle to Wordsworth, a bit south-west. Watch for daffodils if they are in season. (Wordsworth's poem deserves such a planting.)

On your return home, ask yourself at least one question. Why and how did earlier Saskatchewan citizens have the wisdom and knowledge to name so many centres which honour so many masters of the pen? Writers Corner is one proud result.

WILLIAM WORDSWORTH
(1770-1850)

The great Romantic poet born in Cockermouth, (near the Lake District) northern England, remains one of the best-known and most-loved poets of the English language. Before her early death (She died when William was eight and his father died five years later) his mother claimed that her "stiff, moody and violent temper(ed)" son would have a remarkable career for either good or evil. At school, Wordsworth read widely-but just the things he wanted to read-and took long, solitary walks.

After his Cambridge degree, Wordsworth travelled (1791) through revolutionary France and became passionately enthusiastic about events which followed the fall of the Bastille. An ardent republican sympathizer emerged. However, the later Reign of Terror disillusioned him, and a painful period in his life began. While in France he had an affair with Annette Vallon who bore him a daughter, Anne-Caroline. (In 1802 he made a "settlement" with the mother.)

In 1796 his strong friendship began with the poet Samuel Taylor Coleridge and led to their 1798 Lyrical Ballads which opened with Coleridge's famous *The Rime of the Ancient Mariner* and closed with Wordsworth's remarkable *Tintern Abbey*. Wordsworth's reputation soared. His clever sister, Dorothy, became a loyal companion as he moved from place to place.

Wordsworth's increasing interest in the common man showed in his poetry. He was interested in a reinterpretation of nature, of man's relationship to it, and of the relation of both to God. Perhaps more than any other poet, he determined the character of 19th century poetry. In the phrase "On man, on nature, and on human life, musing in solitude" he names the three great themes of poetry. Happiness, he believed, could be found only when the discerning intellect of Man was "wedded to this goodly universe in love and holy passion." Between nature and man he sensed a mysterious bond.

The poet was successful in his conscious attempt to avoid high-flown poetic diction. Instead he used words selected from the common language of "peasants and other humble people."

Coleridge, Southey and Wordsworth are often spoken of as the Lake School because they spent so much of their time there-not far from where Wordsworth was born. There,

Wordsworth lived with his wife, Mary Hutchinson, a gentle, sensible woman, and his sister, Dorothy.

When his friend Robert Southey died in 1843, Wordsworth was named Poet Laureate.

Many readers will recall the poem *My Heart Leaps Up*:

> My heart leaps up when I behold
> A rainbow in the sky:
> So it was when my life began,
> So it is now I am a man,
> So it be when I shall grow old,
> Or let me die!
> The child is father of the Man:
> And I could wish my days to be
> Bound each to each by natural piety.

Perhaps even better known is his sonnet, *Westminister Bridge*.

> Earth has not anything to show more fair;
> Dull would he be of soul who could pass by
> A sight so touching in its majesty:
> The city now doth, like a garment, wear
> The beauty of the morning; silent, bare....

Most impressive is Wordsworth's admonishment of his society in his sonnet *The World is too Much With Us*. When we read this scolding, we can't help but understand that this chastisement is appropriate today in our world of high technology and rush:

> The world is too much with us; late and soon
> Getting and spending, we lay waste our powers:
> Little we see in Nature that is ours;
> We have given our hearts away, a sorded boon!...
>
> For this, for everything we are out of tune;
> It moves us not.—Great god! I'd rather be
> A Pagan suckled in a creed outworn;
> So might I, standing on this pleasant lea,
> Gave glimpses that would make me less forlorn....

Later Wordsworth had his share of critics. Consider Bertrand Russell's comment: "In his youth, Wordsworth sympathized with the French Revolution, went to France, wrote good poetry, and had a natural daughter. At this point he was a "bad" man. Then he became "good", abandoned his daughter, adopted correct principles, and wrote bad poetry."

Earlier Ralph Waldo Emerson (1803-1882), American poet, asked: "Is Wordsworth a bell with a wooden tongue?" And Robert Browning felt that Wordsworth "sold out" to the establishment by becoming poet laureate. "Just for a handful of silver he left us." [and] "Just for a riband to stick in his coat."

Wordsworth was not above being critical in a most dramatic way. He said of William Hazlitt (1778-1830), British essayist: "He is not a proper person to be admitted into respectable society, being the most perverse and malevolent creature that ill-luck had thrown my way." Nor was he to escape abuse. Ezra Pound (1885-1972), American poet reflected in 1913: "Mr. Wordsworth, a stupid man, with a decided gift for portraying nature in vignettes, never yet ruined anyone's morals, unless, perhaps, he has driven some susceptible persons to crime in a very fury of boredom."

As Wordsworth grew older, he became an establishment figure and an ardent patriot. On one occasion the brilliant young poet, John Keats, attempted to break into one of Wordsworth's "monologues." The great man's wife leaned over to Keats and whispered: "Mr. Wordsworth is never interrupted!" He was well known for his lack of humour.

On another occasion, Wordsworth boasted in writer Charles Lamb's presence: "I could write like Shakespeare if I had a mind to." Lamb's soft response: "So it's only the mind that is lacking."

Wordsworth remains a champion of those who affirm the worth, the nobility, the dignity of our common humanity. He loved human decency, plain living, freedom of the spirit, elevated thinking. Life, he tells us, is more than a huddled confusion.

Poet John Keats offered this closing comment: "Wordsworth has left a bad impression wherever he visited in town by his egotism, vanity and bigotry." Thomas Carlyle added about Wordsworth: "For prolixity, thinness, endless dilution, it excels all the other speech I had heard from mortals."

In spite of such criticism, Wordsworth remains the champion of romantic British literature. His finest literature was written in the ten year period ending in 1807. It was the young Wordsworth who produced the poetry admired throughout the world. The following quotes reveal the depth of his thoughts:

-'Tis the still hour of thinking, feeling, loving.
-A brotherhood of venerable trees.
A grandeur in the beatings of the heart.
-Milton! Thou shouldst be living at this hour:
England hath need of thee; she is a fen
Of stagnant waters.
-The cattle are grazing,
Their heads never raising;
There are forty feeding like one!
-The unimaginable touch of time.
-Soft is the music that would charm forever.
-The weight of too much liberty.
-A deep distress hath humanized my soul.
-How is it that you live, and what is it you do?
-Have I not reason to lament
What man has made of man?
-Sometimes sweet, felt in the blood, and felt along the heart.
Poetry is the breath and finer spirit of all knowledge;
It is the impassioned expression which is in the countenance of all science.

-Dread swell of sound! Loud as the gusts that lash
The matted forests of Ontario's shore
By wasteful steel unsmitten.

Does it not seem clear that Wordsworth should be declared capital of Saskatchewpens?

BIBLIOGRAPHY

Adams, George B. and Stephens, H. Morse (Eds.), *Select Documents of English Constitutional History*, New York, Macmillan and Co., Ltd., 1920.

Baker, Alfred, *The Life of Sir Isaac Pitman*, London, Pitman and Sons, 1908.

Bailey, John, *Dr. Johnson And His Circle*, London, Williams & Norgate, 1927.

Boardman, Fon W., *History and Historians*, New York, Henry Z. Walck Inc., 1965.

Bocking D.H. (Ed), *Saskatchewan: A Pictoral History*, Saskatoon, Western Producer Prairie Books, 1980.

Brown, Leonard and Perrin, Porter G (Eds.), *A Quatro of Modern Literature*, New York, Charles Scribner s Sons, 1935.

Byron, May, *A Day with Robert Browning*, London, Hodder and Stoughton, n.d.

Canadian Education: A History, Scarborough, Prentice-Hall of Canada Ltd., 1970.

Cleveland, Charles D., *A Compendium of English Literature*, New York, A.S. Barnes and Co., 1874.

Clurman, Harold, *Ibsen*, New York, Macmillan Publishing Co. Inc., 1977.

Collected Verse of Robert Service, London, Ernest Benn Ltd., 1970.

Colombo, John Robert (Ed), *Colombo s Book of Canada*, Edmonton, Hurtig Publishers, 1978.

Condon, Ann Gorman (Reviewer), A Life of Propriety:Anne Murray Powell and Her Family, 1755-1849 Canadian *Historical Review*, Volume 76, No 4, Dec. 1995.

Cross, Tom Peete, Smith, Reed, Stauffer, Elmer C. and Collette, Elizabeth (Eds.), *English Writers*, Toronto, Ginn and Company, 1959.

Crystal, David, *The Cambridge Factfinder*, New York, Press Syndicate of the University of Cambridge, 1994.

Debus, Allen G. (Ed.), *World Who s Who in Science*, Chicago, A.N. Marquis Co., 1968.

Dictionary of Canadian Biography Vol 1-X1, Toronto, University of Toronto Press, Various dates.

Dictionary of Scientific Biography, Vol XIV, New York, Charles Scribner s Sons, 1976.

Dictionary of the History of Ideas Vol 1-1V, New York, Charles Scribner s Sons, 1973.

Drabble, Margaret (Ed), *The Oxford Companion to English Literature*, Sixth Edition, New York, Oxford University Press, 2000.

Encyclopaedia Britannica, 24 Volumes.

Encyclopedia of World Biography, 22 Volumes, New York, Gale Publishing, 1998.

Fadiman, Clifton (Ed.), *The Little, Brown Book of Anecdotes*, Toronto, Little, Brown and Co., 1985.

Flesch, Rudolph (Ed.), *The Book of Unusual Quotations*, London, Harper & Row, 1957.

Frank, Leonard Roy (Ed), *Random House Websters Wit and Humor Quotationary*, New York, Random House, 2000.

Goldberg, M. Hirsh, *The Book of Lies*, New York, William Morrow & Co. Inc., 1990.

Green, Jonathon (Ed.), *Cassell Dictionary of Insulting Quotations*, London, Cassell, 1999.

Green, Jonathon (ED.), *Cassell Dictionary of Cynical Quotations*, London, Cassell, 1999.

Hacker, Carlotta, *The Book of Canadians*, Edmonton, Hurtig Publishers, 1983.

Hamilton, Robert M., *Canadian Quotations and Phrases*, Toronto, McClelland and Stewart Ltd., 1965.

Hannon, Leslie F. (Ed.), *Canada: Portrait of a Country*, Toronto, McLelland and Stewart Ltd., 1960.

Herbert, Brian (Ed), *Classic Comebacks*, Los Angeles Publishers Inc., 1981.

Knafla, Louis and Klumpenhouwer, Richard, *Lords of the Western Bench*, Edmonton, The Legal Archives Society of Alberta, 1997.

Leggett, Glenn (Ed.), *12 Poets*, Toronto, Holt Rinehart and Winston, 1958.

Lindsay, Joyce and Maurice (Eds.), *The Music Quotation Book*, London, Robert Hale, 1994.

Macdermot, H.E., *Sir Thomas Roddick*, Toronto, Macmillan of Canada, 1938.

McLeod, Jack (Ed.), *The Oxford Book of Canadian Political Anecdotes*, Toronto, Oxford University Press, 1988.

McPhee, Nancy (Ed.), *The Book of Insults*, Markham, Penguin Books, 1978.

Merriam Webster s Encyclopedia of Literature, Springfield, Merriam-Webster Inc. Publishers, 1995.

Metcalf, Fred (Ed.), *The Penguin Dictionary of Modern Humorous Quotations*, (second edition),Toronto, Penguin Books, 2001.

Morton, W.L., *The Kingdom of Canada*, Toronto, McClelland & Steuart Ltd., 1963.

Neider, Charles (Ed.), *The Autobiography of Mark Twain*, New York, Harper and Brothers, 1959.

Olson, Elder, *Major Voices: 20 British and American Poets*, Toronto, McGraw-Hill Book Company, 1973.

Orr, Lyndon, The Story of the Hugos and The Story of the Carlyles *Famous Affinities of History*, London, Harper & Brothers Publishers, 1911.

Panati, Charles, *Panati s Extraordinary Endings of Practically Everything and Everybody*, New York, Harper & Row, 1989.

Peattie, Donald Culross, Mozart: Music s Wonder Child *Lives of Destiny*, New York, The New American Library, 1954.

Pickthall, Marjorie L.C., *The Drift of Pinions*, London, John Lane Company, 1913.

Pickthall, Marjorie L.C., *The Woodcarver s Wife*, Toronto, McClelland and Stewart, 1922.

Piera, Lorne, Marjorie Pickthall: *A Book of Remembrance*, Toronto, Ryerson Press, 1925.

Ratcliff, Susan (Ed.), *The Oxford Dictionary of Thematic Quotations*, New York, Oxford University Press, 2000.

Rees, Nigel (Ed), *Cassell Companion to Quotations,* London, Cassell Publishing Co., 1997.

Rees, Nigel, *The Cassell Dictionary of Anecdotes*, London, Cassell and Co., 1999.

Russell E.T., *What s in a Name,* Calgary, Fifth House Ltd., 1997.

Saldes, George (Ed.), *The Great Thoughts*, New York, Ballantine Books, 1985.

Schwartz, Steven (Ed), *The Seven Deadly Sins*, New York, Gramercy Books, 1997.

Sclanders, Ian, Lucy of Green Gables , *MacLean s.*

Scott, F.R. and Smith AJM (eds.), *The Blasted Pine*, Toronto, The Macmillan Co. of Canada Ltd., 1965.

Sinden, Donald, *The Last Word*, London, Robson Books, 2000.

Stonechild, Blair and Waiser, B:11, *Loyal till Death*, Calgary Fifth House Ltd., 1997.

The Canadian Encyclopedia Vol 1-1V, Edmonton, Hurtig Publishers, 1988.

The Canadian Encyclopedia ,(Second Edition) Four Vols., Edmonton, Hurtig Publishers, 1988.

The Encyclopedia of Philosophy, Vol. 1, London, Collier Macmillan Publishers, 1972.

The Poetical Works of Elizabeth Barrett Browning, (with preparatory memoir), Edinburgh, W.P. Nimmo, Hay, & Mitchell, n.d.

The Saskatchewanians, Published by the Saskatchewan Diamond Jubilee and Canada Centennial Corporation, 1967, n.p.

Wallechinsky, David et al, *The Book of Lists Vols I and II*, New York, William Morrow and Co., Inc., 1978, 1980.

Williams, David Ricardo, *Duff: A Life in the Law*, Vancouver, UBC Press, 1984.

Witherspoon, Alexander M. (Ed.), *The College Survey of English Literature*, New York, Harcourt, Brace and Co., 1951.

Zacks, Richard, *An Underground Education*, New York, Doubleday, 1997.